W9-CCL-461

# U. S.
# Ends and Means in
# Central America

## A Debate

# U.S.
# Ends and Means in
# Central America

## A Debate

ERNEST VAN DEN HAAG

and

TOM J. FARER

PLENUM PRESS • NEW YORK AND LONDON

Library of Congress Cataloging in Publication Data

Van den Haag, Ernest.
    U.S. ends and means in Central America: a debate  /  Ernest van den Haag
and Tom J. Farer.
        p.  cm.
    Bibliography: p.
    Includes index.
    ISBN 0-306-42857-1
    1. Central America — Foreign relations — United States. 2. United States —
Foreign relations — Central America. I. Farer, Tom J. II. Title. III. Title: US
ends and means in Central America.
F1436.U6V36    1988
327.730728 — dc19                                                          87-37689
                                                                                 CIP

Plenum Press is a Division of
Plenum Publishing Corporation
233 Spring Street, New York, N.Y. 10013

Printed in the United States of America

*"I keep my friends as misers do their treasure."*
— PIETRO ARETINO, letter to Giovanni Pollastra,
July 7, 1537 (translated by Samuel Putnam)


To
José Cabranes and Kate Stith
Jack and Kathy Shepherd
Barbara and David Simpson


*Tom J. Farer*

# Preface

What follows is not a work of scholarship but, we hope, one of scholarly analysis and considered opinion that should help to sharpen and structure broad issues of foreign policy for experts and laypersons alike. Virtually all of the facts and theories and opinions to which we refer are in the public domain. For that reason alone it seemed to us that elaborate referencing in footnotes would be otiose. Moreover, while such notes are a prop to credibility in a monologue, the dialectical form of our essay provides a more effective check on any flights of fancy in which we might have been tempted to indulge.

Where we have relied on a particular document, we have so noted in the text. We expect that many readers, provoked by our exchange, will want to deepen their knowledge of the land, culture, politics, and history of Central America, as well as to peruse other opinions, in order to form or test their own instinctive prescriptions for American policy. With them in mind, we have included a selected bibliography of works from all along the political and ideological spectrum.

*Tom J. Farer*
*Ernest van den Haag*

# Acknowledgments

I wish to acknowledge particular debts to Marj Griffin, who helped reproduce the early parts of my contribution and jollied me along all the while, and Jessica Lewis, who, with memorable charm and grace and effort beyond the call of any imaginable professional duty, extracted the Bibliography from the chaos of my files and prepared the Index.

I wish to thank Pergamon Press for permission to include material from my essay "At Sea in Central America: Can We Negotiate Our Way to Shore," which appeared in *Central America: Anatomy of Conflict* (Robert Leiken, ed., 1984), in the initial statement of my case.

I similarly wish to thank *Foreign Policy* and the Carnegie Endowment for International Peace for permission to use, again in my opening statement, material from two articles I originally published in that journal: "Manage the Revolution?" (No. 52, Fall 1983) and "Contadora: The Hidden Agenda" (No. 59, Summer 1985).

*Tom J. Farer*

# Contents

I

CHAPTER 1

# Perspectives
## Moral, Strategic, and Legal

### TOM J. FARER

---

## The Law of the Matter

Lawyers and laymen alike speak of the rule of law in reverential tones. Those of us who have investigated societies where it either has never existed or has collapsed recognize with a peculiar intensity the appropriateness of the tone. When law becomes the whim of the leader or the high command, however initially benign or well-intentioned, we are in the jungle where terror will eventually become a natural state.

As long as we are speaking only of domestic society, no one is likely to dispute this proposition. But when we turn to the society of nations, consensus dissolves. Not only the laity but lawyers as well often disparage the very claim that the relations of states are governed by law. And among those who concede that some law-like process operates on the international plane are many who deny its relevance in cases engaging important or at least allegedly important national interests.

This perceptual separation of the domestic and international realms is evidenced today in the debate over American foreign pol-

3

icy in Central America. That debate is conducted almost exclusively in the idiom of morality and national interest.

Even when law is invoked, it normally appears either as a throwaway argument, the sort you use before a court when you find you have five minutes left in your allotted time and nothing much left to say, or as an unanalyzed and unexplained *ipse dixit*, a mere verbal club.

I suspect that a principal reason, other than ignorance, for failing to use law as a means for orienting ourselves toward this country's Central American policy is a sense that the law is somehow detached from moral and strategic concerns and is, therefore, an insufficient basis for determining where we as individuals ought to stand. Ironically, those most indifferent to the legal position of the parties are often the quickest to employ terms like *aggression*, which, when detached from the world of law, have the same rational force as a punch in the nose. Whether we like it or not, legal concepts, i.e., concepts that have evolved from the actions of states and attendant claims and counterclaims concerning the legitimacy and justness of those actions, have insinuated themselves into our minds, our hearts, and our words, just as our deepest values and interests have inevitably shaped the evolution of those concepts.

Precisely because international law reflects the will of all the parties it governs, rather than being a body of coercive norms imposed by one or a handful of people who may or may not reflect the will of the governed, it must embody shared moral values and strategic interests. To ignore it, therefore, is to ignore the rules and procedures deemed by all states generally to promote their individual ends.

In any legal system, law provides continuity. In that sense, if no other, it tends to protect the interests of those with a stake in the *status quo* and to frustrate revolutionaries—that is, those who wish to manage a sharp break with prevailing norms and institutions and the related distribution of power, wealth, and other values. It would seem to follow, then, that the United States, as the richest, most powerful, and most influential state, has a particular interest in upholding the rule of international law. And that is sufficient reason for a patriot, committed to advancing our national interests, to feel concern about the decision of the Reagan administration to reject the jurisdiction of the International Court of Justice in the case brought against us by the government of Nicaragua. Concern about this unilateral denial of jurisdiction is shared by those who believe that the court erred in finding that it had jurisdiction and that, in any event, the United States had a winning case on the merits, and by those who think that the Court's jurisdictional finding was reasonable and that the United States properly lost on the merits.

After all, one of the general principles of law, at least in the West, is that a court has the power to determine its jurisdiction. Of course, if in the instant case there were evidence that the Court had been corrupted or coerced, one would feel differently. In fact, even the most fervent advocates of the administration's position have suggested nothing of the kind.

Before withdrawing from the case, the United States argued that the Central American conflict was essentially a political question and hence beyond the jurisdiction of the World Court. The Court, including its distinguished Western members, rejected that contention, in my judgment rightly. The fundamental constitutional document of the contemporary international system is the United Nations Charter. I think it hard to disagree with the proposition that the principal purpose of the charter, of the norms it announced and the institutions it established, was regulating and limiting the use of force. The charter speaks directly to the issue of when force may legitimately be employed—namely, in self-defense and, conversely, never in ways that threaten the political independence and territorial integrity of any state.

The Nicaraguan claim rests directly on an alleged violation of the charter. The Court's jurisdiction extends to cases arising out of treaties—the charter is, of course, a treaty—and since it was established coincident with the establishment of the United Nations and interrelates functionally with the institution, one may reasonably assume that the founding fathers regarded the Court as one of the linchpins of the new system. Since the overriding purpose of the new system, as I have already pointed out, was restraining the use of force in international relations, it would seem that if the Court were to have jurisdiction over any issue, it would be that one.

The U.S. position, as I understand it, is that while the Court may be authorized to consider disputes before they erupt into armed conflict, once conflict has broken out, only the Security Council has jurisdiction. There is force to that argument, if the council is indeed functioning. But it plainly was not functioning at the time the United States challenged the Court's jurisdiction, in part because, by an earlier veto, the United States had indicated that it would not tolerate Security Council review of its actions against the Nicaraguan government. For the United States to invoke the putatively exclusive jurisdiction of the council after having disabled the council is, to say the least, amusing.

I turn now to the merits. As counsel for the state department, I have argued roughly as follows. The government of Nicaragua is in some measure aiding an armed rebellion against the recognized government of El Salvador. Since the rebels have not been recognized explicitly by any government (including the government of Nicaragua) as a movement equivalent in legitimacy to the Duarte regime, other states are not entitled under international law to aid them, just as all states *are* entitled to aid Duarte and his colleagues. Thus, Nicaragua cannot justify its behavior on the grounds that it is responding to prior illegal acts by the United States and other countries, such acts being the military assistance extended to the Duarte government.

Unless and until the rebels are widely recognized as belligerents and the conflict as a classic civil war, aid to the rebels is an act of aggression. Within the terms of the U.N. charter it is an "armed attack," entitling the friends of El Salvador to join it in acts of collective self-defense.

As part of the self-defense effort the United States has organized, armed, and supplied opponents of the Nicaraguan government, the so-called Contras. Aid to the Contras being in pursuit of Salvadoran security, it is legitimate as long as it complies with the classic principles of proportionality and exhaustion of less peace-threatening remedies. Our response is clearly proportional to the delinquency, since that delinquency is properly defined as collusion in a sustained, powerful, and comprehensive effort to overthrow a legitimate government. We have, moreover, resorted to force only after failing through negotiations, threats, and economic inducements to terminate the violation of Salvadoran sovereignty. To be sure, negotiations are episodically renewed. Their renewal is a sign of our good faith. But so far they have proved fruitless, because the Nicaraguan government is intransigently committed to a revolution without frontiers.

There, in essence, is the U.S. case. It is sufficiently respectable so that a lawyer could present it without embarrassment. But in the end it fails to persuade me either as an application of existing international law or as an implicit claim about what the law ought to allow. Both considerations of policy and canons of construction cast doubt on the claim that virtually any level and kind of assistance to rebels allows other states to treat such assistance as the legal equivalent of an armed attack. Since aid to rebels is such a persistent feature of the contemporary state system with its porous borders and transnational sympathies, is it reasonable to construe a charter designed above all to limit conflict as allowing states to expand an essentially domestic conflict into an international one, except in cases where cross-border aid is an important, if not essential, element in triggering or sustaining rebellion against duly constituted authorities?*

Of course, the Reagan administration has alleged that Nicaraguan aid is essential for maintaining the Salvadoran opposition as a serious threat to the Duarte government. But despite plausible

---

*In its subsequent decision, the Court by an overwhelming majority answered this question in the negative.

claims by United States intelligence that it can determine when a
toilet flushes in Managua, the evidence adduced by the administration to substantiate its allegations about the levels of Nicaraguan aid
has been meager. This is, nevertheless, a question of fact that could
have been presented to the World Court. The argument that we
would have been hopelessly constrained by the need to protect intelligence sources is not wholly convincing because most of the
sources are doubtless technological in character rather than secret
agents and much of the technology of intelligence-gathering is practically in the public domain. Furthermore, we would not have had
to expose every grain of evidence to make our case. Surely if the
Nicaraguan aid levels are as high as the administration implies,
there ought to be a rich cornucopia of evidence from which we
could draw sufficient nuggets to satisfy any reasonable evidential
burden.

Be that as it may, the more serious objection to the administration's legal position is its claim to have exhausted measures short of
current levels of force. That claim would be persuasive if we were
offering to terminate aid to the "Contras" in exchange for verifiable guarantees from the Sandinistas to terminate all forms of aid to
the Salvadoran opposition. Under existing international law that is
all we have a right to demand. In an effort to circumvent this difficulty, the administration has sometimes alleged that the only secure
guarantee of compliance would be the existence of a totally open
political system in Nicaragua.

For moral reasons, I would love to see such a system flourish-
ing in that sad country. But the claimed connection between verification, on the one hand, and free press and an effective political
opposition, on the other, is far too speculative to sustain the administration's legal argument. Exposés long after the fact have demonstrated the capacity of fully democratic governments like our own
or those of Western Europe to carry out extensive intelligence operations in secrecy and in peacetime. But for the Watergate burglary,
for instance, even today we would probably know nothing about the

assassination plots and other operations conducted by the Central Intelligence Agency. Conversely, despite its restraints on the press and other deviations from the democratic model, Nicaragua because of its position is a porous and penetrable place and will remain so even if its government takes a still more authoritarian turn.

For at least two years Managua has been sending signals indicating its readiness to trade revolutionary fraternity throughout Central America for United States tolerance of the revolution in Nicaragua. Contemporary international law requires the United States to test the *bona fides* of that offer. By upping the ante, by demanding power sharing in Managua (which may be a mere preliminary to an effort to eliminate the Sandinistas altogether), the United States has stepped outside the domain of legal justification as well as estranging itself from the Contadora powers.

Can it nevertheless be argued that the United States is acting in a manner consistent with the nature of a decentralized legal system where new law can be made only by pushing hard against the boundaries of the old law? That would depend, I take it, on whether United States behavior can be framed in terms of general principles we are prepared to allow enemies as well as friends to invoke. Particularly in the past year or two, the president has implied that producing democracy in Nicaragua is an end in itself justifying the use of force.

Like Mario Vargas Llosa, the eminent Peruvian writer, I find it hard to imagine democracy taking root in the ruins left after a U.S.-orchestrated invasion of Nicaragua. But putting aside the question of plausible connection between the president's ends and the available means, is he in fact claiming that military interventions to create democracies should be treated as exceptions to the general prohibition of aggression? In a world where most governments are not democratic, such a norm could never win much support and therefore cannot by its nature be anything more than a challenge to the very existence of a system of law among nations. Moreover, it is doubtful, very doubtful, that we as a people are prepared to act on the basis of the norm except where the non-democratic regime is unfriendly to the United States or one of its allies. If we were prepared to intervene in Paraguay and South Africa, as well as Nicaragua, and remain in occupation the many long years required to construct a democratic system with any hope of surviving our departure, the norm would have at least *moral* allure.

The administration's rhetoric implies another claim that can be given legal form—namely, that a certain sort of revolutionary regime is by its nature threatening to its neighbors and they are therefore entitled to eliminate it preemptively. This is, of course, somewhat (and hence disturbingly) analogous to the view the Soviet Union takes of non-Leninist parties of reform in Eastern Europe. In any event, it represents such an extension of the concept of self-defense that the term must become entirely subjective. And so it leads us back to the legal universe before the Second World War when force was simply the conduct of diplomacy by other means. Being a great, civilized, and essentially satisfied power, our interests are unlikely to be best served by the re-creation of a Hobbesian jungle where the rule of law has ceased altogether to restrain violence among states.

While I appreciate that Professor van den Haag may not agree with my analysis, I hope he will nevertheless concur that approaching the conflict in Central America from a legal perspective does help to sharpen the issues and to provide a framework encouraging to the open, informed, and mutually tolerant debate that is the hallmark of a democratic society.

## Legitimate Ends and Dubious Means

Negotiations can serve either to promote compromise or to confirm defeat. This deep ambiguity has allowed President Reagan to claim without mendacity that, no less than the critics of his policies in Central America, he favors negotiations. For clearly he is prepared at any time to negotiate the surrender of the Sandinista government. That end being nonnegotiable, at the moment, the president must pursue it through other means.

The administration's compulsion to batter chosen opponents into submission is a sad spectacle because it augurs further suffering for the people of Central America, already mutilated by a terrible history in which the United States has played a conspicuous part. This compulsion is also paradoxical. Normally, self-interest is the force that drives the leaders of one state to impose agony on the people of another. In this instance, any rational definition of self-interest dictates a policy of compromise. A second paradox springs from the president's claim to be animated not merely by a parochial conception of national interest but also by concern for the men, women, and children of Nicaragua and other countries being sucked into the vortex of regional war. When enumerating his objectives, President Reagan speaks of human rights and democracy in the same breath that invokes threats to United States security. Yet the only possible means of reconciling the humane with the strategic is through the very compromises that administration seems to eschew—compromises that his own policies may have made possible.

There lies the final and most bitter paradox, that of a president, blinded by ideology, who will not reap what he has sown. Seven years ago the Sandinista comandantes apparently envisioned Nicaragua as the asylum, command point, and entrepôt of an isthmus-wide revolution. Now they seem prepared, if not eager, to negotiate pacts of mutual tolerance with their neighbors; they seem, in other words, to have arrived at a point of convergence with the United States objectives announced by President Carter and at least nominally adopted by his successor. However, as revolutionary forces have reduced their appetite, ours apparently has grown.

The Reagan administration originally justified military aid to opponents of the Sandinista regime, the so-called Contras, as a means to cut off the arms supply to the Salvadoran guerillas. In this connection the administration urged the notion of symmetry. Such aid would help the enemies of the government in Managua as long as that government helped the enemies of our "friends" in San Salvador. But now, having dined on the first course of its campaign to make Managua more pliable, and having found the eating good, the administration apparently wants the Sandinistas to serve up something more than an enforceable commitment to neutrality. And that something is themselves.

In April 1983, the then-assistant secretary of state, Thomas Enders, told the Senate Foreign Relations Committee: "Central American democrats...are particularly clear on the need for democratization [in the region]. Only in this way could they be confident they will not have to face sometime in the future an aggressive neighbor unconstrained by the limits democracy imposes." Three months later a senior U.S. diplomat based in Central America informed Christopher Dickey of *The Washington Post* that issues other than the question of aid to the insurgents in El Salvador probably could not be negotiated successfully with the Sandinistas until they change their approach to government. He added: "It is now considered that the only way they can be trusted to keep an agreement is to have the type of government which would force them to do so or make it a public issue."

The administration dispelled any lingering doubts about its objectives when it brushed aside the package of proposals presented by the Nicaraguan government on October 2, 1983. Unlike proposals of a more general character that Managua had made in 1982, the subsequent package included detailed provisions designed to assuage Washington's anxieties concerning aid to possible revolutionary movements and Soviet or Cuban use of military facilities in Nicaragua.

Pursuant to the proposed treaty with the United States, Nicaragua would pledge that "it will not permit [its territory] to be utilized to affect or to threaten the security of the United States or to attack any other state." Nicaraguan foreign minister Miguel d'Escoto said the agreements required his country to dismantle any command and control facilities on Nicaraguan soil that might exist for use by Salvadoran guerrilla groups to coordinate the movement of their forces inside El Salvador and to arrange for supply shipments. More significant than these verbal commitments is the Nicaraguan government's declared willingness to allow on-site observation as a means of policing compliance. To be sure, the draft treaty in this package directed specifically to the conflict in El Salvador treats the regime and its opponents as equals and even-handedly prohibits aid to both.

If, as a decreasing number of observers believe, the Salvadoran security forces would disintegrate without constant infusions of U.S. aid (even if the guerrillas were also cut off from external suppliers), the treaty in its proposed form was unsatisfactory. But it would be an odd diplomacy indeed if a country initiated negotiations by conceding all of its opposite number's demands. So the inclusion of reciprocal restraints in what the Nicaraguan government simply called a basis for negotiations does not satisfactorily explain their back-of-the-hand reception in Washington, particularly in light of the administration's insistence on the significance of external aid to the Salvadoran guerrillas.

The administration's refusal either to accept the proposals as a basis for negotiation or to table any alternative negotiating package reenforced the impression that Washington seeks to alter the Nicaraguan regime itself rather than its external policies.

On their face, demands for the democratization of Nicaraguan politics are not equivalent to proposals for a unilateral suicide pact. The statements quoted above could be interpreted as envisioning continued Sandinista preeminence coincident with an institutionalized and secure opposition. One feels, nevertheless, that to the extent the Reagan administration has anything very specific in mind, it must be more than that. If the United States is demanding democratization merely to secure monitors of Sandinista compliance with a no-export-of-revolution agreement, the demand seems gratuitous. It seems gratuitous, first, because the administration's indictment of Nicaraguan aid to the Salvadoran rebels rests on its own claimed capability to monitor Managua's behavior. Second, although the opposition is harassed and censored, as I noted earlier, the country remains so porous that there is little of significance that happens there that is not quickly and widely known both within and beyond its frontiers.

If a secure political opposition cannot heighten the already high risk of exposure—should the Sandinistas violate a nonintervention commitment—surely something more than exposure is at stake. Must the opposition have a permanent veto on the government's foreign policy in order to mitigate Washington's distrust? That would be a curious constitutional provision, one with little or no parallel in the known world. Even if such a provision existed on paper, would it deter a regime willing to risk exposure and consequent retaliation from the United States? As a practical matter, the only consistently effective domestic political restraint is the threat of electoral defeat. So Washington's linkage of democratization and nonintervention logically implies an opposition that, by means of exposure, can hope to win an election and replace the Sandinista government.

Sandinista acceptance of a competitive political system would not be suicidal. The comandantes still appear to enjoy significant support, particularly among younger, urban Nicaraguans. A government wholly reliant on the terror its security forces could impose would not distribute arms broadly among the civil population, as the government in Managua has done. In progressively diminished form this support has survived conflict with the Catholic Church, economic privation, and betrayal of the original commitment to nonalignment in international affairs. In opening the political system the Sandinistas would concomitantly reduce their electoral liabilities, because the decision to open would be taken as part of a larger decision to pursue reconciliation with the democratic opposition. To achieve reconciliation, the government of Managua would have to make peace with the Catholic Church, lift restrictions on press and speech, give amnesty to political prisoners, and offer attractive concessions to the Miskito Indians and other minorities. These steps, plus the removal of U.S. economic sanctions, could create the climate of confidence essential to reverse the outflow of capital and managerial talent, and might thus fuel economic growth. Once unencumbered by conflict with the Church and a shrinking economy, the comandantes—with their far-flung organization, populist program, newspaper, and residual mystique as military leaders of the national revolution—would present a powerful electoral force, assuming they remained united. The Sandinistas' potential ability to win an electoral competition makes the U.S. demand for democratization something less, at least in form, than insistence that the comandantes self-destruct.

With the Reagan administration dangling the seductive image of an emergent social democracy in Nicaragua, moderates and liberals have found it difficult to unite in opposition to the president's actual policies. Americans who cheered the Nicaraguan revolution have felt betrayed by the subsequent course of events, rather as if they were personally responsible for the overthrow of Anastasio Somoza. President Reagan has played on that feeling, even claiming ignorantly that the Sandinistas violated a kind of legal commitment to install multiparty democracy.

The truth, of course, is that the United States contributed to the revolution only by doing nothing decisive to block it. A faction within the Carter administration did urge positive steps to force Somoza out, but it lost every battle. With characteristic amnesia, many Americans have forgotten the Carter administration's determined effort, initiated at the first sign of Somoza's weakness, to assemble an anti-Sandinista coalition, including the civilian apparatus of the Somoza regime, with a sanitized National Guard as its chopping edge. If successful, that effort would probably have produced war without end to defend Somocismo without Somoza.

Whether wise or foolish, the Carter administration's actual behavior during Somoza's last year can hardly be squared with the

proposition that, in consideration of U.S. aid in defanging Somoza, the Sandinistas assumed an obligation to institutionalize-
democracy.

Of course the United States should have deployed its political
and economic resources to accelerate Nicaragua's transformation.
If it had, several tens of thousands of people now dead would be
alive. Today Nicaragua would probably be governed by a coalition,
including the Sandinistas, committed to nonalignment in foreign
affairs and, domestically, to reform within a capitalist framework.

I rake over the past only because its coals still burn among us.
Americans committed to the promotion of democratic values everywhere in the hemisphere should arraign authoritarian rule in
Nicaragua. We would therefore be right to support the administration's policies if there were still a credible basis for believing that,
at reasonable cost to our national interest and the people of
Nicaragua, these policies were likely to promote a democratic outcome. Today, such a belief must rest on faith alone.

Had the promotion of human rights been its main concern, the
administration's strategy—organizing a military force to challenge
the Sandinista government and threatening direct military intervention—would from the outset have seemed a wild gamble. For such
a strategy could succeed only if the comandantes responded to the
military challenge by offering their opponents a nonviolent route to
power. Yet historical experience suggests that military threats create an environment peculiarly inclement for political participation
or any other kind of human right. As administration ideologues
have been quick to point out when defending the delinquencies
of right-wing regimes, subversion aggravates the endemic paranoia
of authoritarian regimes, leading them to impose a tighter grip on
society. Whatever capacity they once had for distinguishing dissent
from treason rapidly atrophies. By driving moderates underground
where they join the violent opposition, the crackdown further
polarizes society, eroding conditions necessary for a politics of-
accommodation.

Nicaragua's government is conditioned by history and ideology to view the United States as an irreducibly hostile power regardless of who occupies the oval office. Its occupation by a leader of the American right naturally strengthens the belief that the United States will attempt to liquidate any government of the left in the Western Hemisphere, even an elected one. Opposition movements tied politically and militarily to the United States will be seen as means to United States ends and, hence, irreconcilable. Thus, concessions appear not only useless but dangerous. Concessions imply recognition of opponents as a substantial political force, a legitimate claimant to rights of participation in the national political order. Once endowed with such legitimacy, a movement is better positioned to invite intervention on its behalf, since intervention by invitation of a substantial, indigenous actor is less quickly characterized as aggression. The strategic dilemma, then, is that the added leverage any opposition group acquires against the Nicaraguan regime by virtue of United States support is offset by the tendency of that support to convince the regime of the disutility of compromise.

Among its many virtues, power sharing in Managua would turn the edge of the United States argument for symmetry in dealing with El Salvador and Nicaragua. I once concluded a private talk with Tomas Borge and Daniel Ortega with the warning: "Remember, you have an opportunity to make a unique contribution to fascism in Latin America. To guarantee its ascendancy, to doom hope for reform, all you have to do is force this national revolution into an authoritarian mold." The obverse also remains true: The successful emergence in Nicaragua of a political order as committed to freedom as it is to reform would shake the very foundations of neighboring authoritarian states. In this historical moment, the force of example is greater than the example of force. Believing as they do in the efficacy of raw power, President Reagan and his aides probably are constitutionally disabled from envisioning the ripple effect of a democracy in Nicaragua. Unfortunately, the Sandinistas seem to suffer equally from lack of imagination.

By not being consciously pursued, the strategy has had its best possible test. The Sandinistas know that Washington has not been seeking to induce reconciliation with social democrats and democratic conservatives and a consequent social democracy in Nicaragua. They believe that Reagan seeks not to reform but rather to destroy their regime. They take his threats seriously and are therefore prepared to make concessions, but not concessions concerning the distribution of government offices that would amount to an immediate sharing of power. The United States has now done almost everything but invade. It has failed to pry open the regime. One can conclude that military pressure will not bring democracy to Nicaragua.

The democratic promise of present policy being slight, the United States should try one less costly in the currency of both human rights and national interest and one that, coincidently, is more likely to succeed.

A first objection to current policy is that it kills people and promises to kill many more. Although the Contras seem unable to pose a truly serious military challenge to the Sandinistas, they have managed to kill several thousand supporters and employees of the government, and private persons, and doubtless have suffered substantial casualties of their own. We are not doing the killing ourselves. But without United States financial support and training, and without the hope of an ultimate ride to victory on the back of a United States invasion force, and without the United States guarantee of Honduras's security, which in turn produces a Honduran sanctuary, the Contras' capacity to wage war would be greatly reduced.

A second objection is the effect of current policy on the democratic prospects elsewhere in Central America, particularly Honduras. In the course of turning that country into an American base for operations against the Sandinistas, the United States has fostered the polarization of Honduran politics.

A third objection is the policy's capacity to distract both the

Congress and the executive branch from intrinsically more important issues.

A fourth objection is the risk of igniting and then sucking the United States into a regional war. The Honduran armed forces, made cocky by U.S. backing and eager to take on Nicaragua, might arrange some extreme provocation—for example, crossing the border on the pretext of a prior Nicaraguan incursion—then invoking United States guarantees. Or Honduran and Contra troops, possibly reenforced by Guatemalan and Salvadoran units, might drive into Nicaragua, set up a provisional government, secure recognition from the conspiring regimes, and then, when threatened with destruction by Nicaraguan armed forces, launch an appeal our right-wing president might find hard to resist.*

A fifth objection is the policy's power to reinforce the image of the United States, so current among the educated youth of Latin America, as the implacable foe of social change, an image that helped shape the mentality of the relatively young men and women who now govern Nicaragua. An administration that, until the recent escalation of its anti-Sandinista campaign, sought pleasant relations with every right-wing thug in the hemisphere is simply unconvincing when it claims to be struggling for democracy in Central America.

A final objection to continuation of the present policy is the availability of an alternative more likely to produce the desired result. The Sandinistas have established nothing like totalitarian control over Nicaragua, not because of United States opposition but rather because of the nature of Nicaraguan society and, *possibly*, of their own movement.

The great mass of the population is Catholic and socially conservative. As an opponent of Somoza during the national rising, the Church avoided any taint from the old order. On the contrary, the Church enjoys the prestige of participation in the liberation strug-

---

*In the wake of the Iran–Contra hearings, this scenario is far less plausible.

gle. Whatever their ideology and ambitions, the comandantes have no hope of eliminating this powerful institutional expression of pluralistic values.*

Geographic position is an additional obstacle to the perpetuation of rigid, authoritarian rule. Nicaragua, like all the Caribbean basin, is inevitably subject to the magnetic force of American culture, as it is doomed to dependence on American markets. The country has neither the size nor the resources nor the trained cadres to run an autarchic economic system. Furthermore, the Soviet Union has indicated plainly that it is not prepared to assume responsibility for yet another welfare case. This fact alone distinguishes the Cuban precedent. By withdrawing the military threat, Washington would itself establish a second decisive distinction. For then, the Sandinistas, unlike Castro, could not portray themselves as nationalist heroes facing down the regional Goliath. In this respect, current U.S. policy plays into Sandinista hands, creating a drama in which they can star.

The country's cultural and institutional heritage, together with its geographic position and economic necessities, will exert continuing and ultimately effective pressures for a plural political order, even if the United States is passive. Ending the U.S. military threat to the Sandinista regime does not, however, entail passivity. We could continue to deploy economic sanctions and incentives. The Sandinistas need access to American capital and markets, as well as private sector confidence, in order to deliver promised economic and social progress. A conservative president is peculiarly well positioned to extract from Congress the kind and quantity of economic carrots capable of influencing political developments in Nicaragua. Economic cooperation conditioned neither on Nicaragua's openness to United States investors nor on Chicago School economics but rather on its respect for human rights, including the right to participate in government, will augment the internal

*This is, to be sure, an ironic reversal of the Church's traditional role in Latin American States.

forces advocating democratic reform. If not tied to conservative theology, United States efforts are more likely to attract reinforcing action from democratic governments in Europe and Latin America.

Such a policy does not promise immediate results and cannot guarantee success. For the American Right, it will never have the charm of military force with its false promise of decisive consequences. American forces thinly covered by the Contra fig leaf could, if committed in large numbers, successfully invade Nicaragua and occupy its major cities. They could not, in the foreseeable future, pacify either the urban barrios or the countryside. Instead, the United States would incur costs out of proportion even to the most demented conception of the national interest and extract an unspeakable toll in human rights.

The Sandinistas clearly have a substantial social base. In case of invasion, nationalists, including some present opponents of the regime, would join in defending the country. Faced with determined resistance the United States would use its vast fire power. Those Nicaraguans who collaborated in the resulting holocaust would encounter extraordinary difficulties in trying to construct democracy amidst the blood-soaked ruins of their country. This option continues, nevertheless, to lurk in the background of contemporary policy.

Though it has not succeeded in producing democracy in Nicaragua, administration policy has apparently convinced the Nicaraguan government of the need to allay United States security concerns. Now is the time to negotiate the sort of compromise settlement the former assistant secretary of state, Thomas Enders, apparently offered the Sandinistas almost four years ago, before our appetite grew. Managua would agree to neutralize itself: no military relations with Cuba or the Soviet Union; no assistance to Central American rebels; no army out of proportion in size or quality of weapons to those of its neighbors.

By agreeing to respect Nicaragua's neutral status the United States would offer no further support for the various Contra groups, would withdraw troops from and terminate military aid to Honduras, and would encourage Honduran participation in the neutralization negotiations. This agreement is roughly what the Contadora states (Panama, Mexico, Colombia, and Venezuela) have attempted to achieve. Negotiations would be carried out under their auspices and would include all the Central American states and the United States. In light of Cuba's declared sympathy for the Contadora framework, and the utility of obtaining its formal commitment to the terms of any settlement, Cuba should be invited to participate.

Since, at the urging of the Contadora group, democratization has already been accepted by all the Central American states as one of the bases for a settlement, it should be an issue in the negotiations. As things stand now, a precise enumeration of steps for converting that principle into practice probably cannot be obtained. However, the principle itself should be incorporated in the ultimate substantive agreements, as a latent benchmark of legitimacy.* In addition, the United States should in conjunction with the Contadora states and their support group (Argentina, Brazil, Peru, and Uruguay) offer generous material incentives for Sandinista acceptance of leaders of the armed opposition, other than those guilty of collaboration with the Somoza regime, as participants in the negotiating process.

Being representative of important sectors in Nicaraguan society, their inclusion is important both to the prospects for peace and to the opening of Nicaraguan politics. Moreover, the United States should attach to the agreements a declaration that it has become a party to them on the assumption (1) that as the military threat to Managua diminishes, the human rights situation in that country, documented by reports of the Inter-American Commission on Human Rights and other credible bodies, will correspondingly improve, and (2) that the Managua government remains committed to a progressive opening of the political system. Furthermore, the

---

*As it has been in the so-called Arias proposal signed by the Central American presidents in September 1987.

United States should insist that the agreements include a commitment from Managua for amnesty for *all* members of the opposition not accused of specific atrocities during the Somoza period or during the present conflict, and willing to renounce the use of force. Finally, all parties to the agreements would undertake to strengthen existing protections and guarantees of human rights in their respective countries, including the right to free expression of political views.

## The Contadora Factor

A seeming contradiction lies at the heart of the approach of the Contadora group (Colombia, Mexico, Panama, and Venezuela) toward the conflict in Central America. All four members oppose the proliferation of Soviet-style regimes in the Western Hemisphere, all four would prefer to see a more open political system in Nicaragua, and none would welcome a radical revolutionary triumph in El Salvador. Yet all not only steadfastly oppose United States military intervention to achieve these goals but also worry about the Reagan administration's depiction of Central America as one front in the global confrontation between East and West. And they are frightened by the degree to which their backyards have already been militarized.

These disagreements with Washington concern far more than the relative efficacy of different policy tools or an interesting academic dispute over the origins of turmoil in the region. Instead, they reflect a judgment by the Contadora countries that current United States policies threaten their futures more than do radical forces in the small countries of Central America. Specifically, they fear that even a direct United States military intervention that liquidated the armed Left in El Salvador and drove the Sandinistas into the mountains would be far more likely to destroy their own fragile political orders than the triumph and survival of revolutionaries in two comparatively unimportant Central American countries. Understanding why the Contadora countries feel this way is the first step toward a more realistic United States policy in the region.

The centrist elites that rule the Contadora countries view the comparatively open frameworks they have built as their best hope for preserving their own power base, as well as sparing their countries the agony of civil strife. They feel secure enough to withstand the reverberations of nearby revolutions. But they are convinced that full-scale war in Central America would upset the balance of interests that is the sole guarantor of their moderate political orders. By ignoring these calculations, the United States has put itself on a collision course with countries that share its security concerns and that could be useful partners.

The relatively mild and relatively open political orders of the Contadora states are nonetheless brittle. They are neither powerfully institutionalized—with the possible exception of Mexico—nor cushioned by a widely accepted democratic ethos and idiom. For important groups in all of these countries, the rule of law (*estado del derecho*), competitive politics, and other aspects of human rights are essentially means for promoting their own interests, not transcendent ends. And other groups, which currently acquiesce in rule by centrist elites, plainly chafe under these restraints, awaiting opportunities to break free. The Center holds, but precariously.

Evidence of fragility in these countries abounds. In Colombia, militarization of the judicial system and other deviations from democracy were reported in 1980 and 1981 by Amnesty International and the Inter-American Commission on Human Rights. The "creeping coup," as some Colombians called these developments, was not just the army's idea. Although part of the traditional governing elite urged the incorporation of new groups demanding access to political power, another segment demanded firmness in the face of threats. The bitter dispute within both traditional parties— Liberals and Conservatives—over a general amnesty and concurrent negotiations with guerrilla leaders exemplified the centrifugal forces threatening a moderate political order.

In Mexico, a striking sign of the uneasiness of the civilian political elite was the fiercely nationalistic government's remarkably low-key response to the Guatemalan army's repeated raids miles into Mexico to kidnap refugees suspected of guerrilla connections. The government's restraint stemmed at least partly from fear that a major diplomatic confrontation would heighten pressure for military participation in policy making. Another even clearer sign of tension is the continuing harassment of opposition political parties despite their potential utility for the peaceful channeling of discontent.

Ideological wars in neighboring countries threaten these fairly conciliatory, progressively more inclusive political orders and buttress the advocates of closure by force. They dramatize issues concerning the distribution of wealth and power that the Contadora states, to varying degrees, have managed to mute. The threat of war tends to give these issues a dangerous, renewed prominence. Moreover, a feeling of ideological fraternity and practical interest in exploiting the emotions aroused and sharpened by the neighboring conflict invariably encourage both poles of the political spectrum to indict the Center's instinctive neutrality, thereby adding yet another issue to the agenda of latent internecine conflict.

As long as the conflict is localized, however, the centrist Contadora establishments seem able to manage these pressures. But they would prefer not to face them at all. Therefore, they will support the emergence of political orders that, like their own, can produce enough change, distribute enough income or opportunity, or coopt enough members of the potential counterelite to evade entrapment in the Procrustean alternatives of hideous repression and civil war. These fears are never openly admitted by the Contadora regimes, for governments rarely advertise their structural weaknesses. But in private conversations, the anxieties shared by these elites are clear.

Deep United States involvement in Central America's civil wars would accentuate the centrifugal forces always threatening to rip apart political order in the Contadora states and in their Central American sibling, Costa Rica, even if Washington scrupulously avoided efforts to align the Contadora governments with its policy aims. Significant segments of the educated elite throughout the Caribbean Basin are animated by any major American initiative. The long history of United States involvement in their countries' destinies; the deep infiltration of American culture into their lives; the dense economic networks on which individual, family, and national well-being depend; and the profusion of personal ties and personal experiences (for example, Disneyland, Bloomingdale's, and the Inter-American Defense College) generate on the Right an instinctive deference to Washington's preferences and perspectives and on the Left an instinctive hostility. Once galvanized by a local American initiative, both factions pressure their governments to pursue a foreign policy consistent with their incompatible preferences, thereby underscoring and intensifying their endemic hostility and shaking the foundations of tolerance.

Since the United States, like any other state, will try to marshal diplomatic support and to neutralize potential opposition among regional actors, the decision to intervene anywhere in the region entails more subtle, but potentially destabilizing, forms of intervention everywhere in the region. America unavoidably becomes an active participant in the domestic politics of each state, driven by its objectives and its points of leverage—particularly the military or people in business who are either export-oriented or linked with U.S. corporations— to collaborate with the Right and to inflame the Left. In addition, Washington is continually tempted to apply pressure directly on the governing centrist coalition—as some advisors urged President Reagan to do at the height of the Mexican financial crisis.

The consequent domestic polarization is best illustrated by Honduras, whose fragile semidemocracy nearly collapsed under the weight of American determination to turn the country into a base for operations supporting El Salvador and opposing Nicaragua.

Power within the military tilted toward General Gustavo Alvarez Martinez and his colleagues, who composed the faction that was most belligerent, most authoritarian, most closely tied to extremist business leaders (this faction also had connections with the Reverend Sun Myung Moon), and most eager to convert the country into an American subsidiary. Rightist paramilitary units and leftist guerrillas suddenly leaped onto the hitherto quiet local stage. The phenomenon of disappeared persons made its now predictable appearance. One could see more than the end of the country's flirtation with democracy; one could see Honduras slipping for the first time into the nightmare world of private and public terrorism.

The country's remission, initiated by the military's expulsion of Alvarez, resulted in part from the general's quirky character and, according to press reports too numerous to be discounted, the imperiousness of United States Ambassador John Negroponte, whom many in Honduras believed better suited for the British Colonial Service in the days when its representatives ruled over more than a few large rocks. The experience of Honduras also suggests that even in a desperately poor, vulnerable country, ideas of national dignity and interest limit American influence.

Honduras's longer-term future is still uncertain. But the country remains an illustration of the dangers to domestic equilibrium that the Contadora states have been attempting to avoid by confning Central America's violence and discounting its alleged ideological and geopolitical significance.

A related motive behind Contadora, at least for the more progressive elements in each country's governing coalition, undoubtedly is concern for the message that would be sent by the repression of the Salvadoran rebels, unaccompanied by significant reform, which would be the likeliest result of total victory over the insurgents. As their United States and West European counterparts have done since their own welfare states emerged, Contadora elites are debating how much reform is necessary to maintain calm among the popular classes. If El Salvador ultimately demonstrates that the traditional United States guarantee of survival in the event of elite miscalculation is still good and that Nicaragua is an anomaly, the position of those who discount the need for substantial concessions will be reinforced.

It is true, however, that collapse of the Salvadoran military and the emergence of a ferociously vengeful and radically redistributive government would inevitably heighten the paranoia of the wealthier classes and thereby augment the ranks of the far Right in all the Contadora states. This was precisely the effect throughout the hemisphere of Fidel Castro's triumph in Cuba. The sudden prestige acquired by the armed Left produced a spiral of violence that left most of Latin America in the hands of governments pursuing rigidly conservative ends with ruthlessly immoderate means.

Centrist elites in the Contadora states apparently are betting that, at least for the short term, the United States will supply enough aid to prevent an outright rebel victory. In the meantime, these elites seek United States and West European support for efforts to manage a settlement without victors—the only outcome they believe will not strain but rather will reinforce their own political systems.

At root, however, it is fear of direct U.S. intervention that has shifted Colombia, Panama, and Venezuela away from their traditional posture of compliance with American policy; moved Colombia to raise its low diplomatic profile; and propelled the traditional lone wolf, Mexico, into coalition diplomacy. Also cementing the Contadora states into a coherent diplomatic agent has been the shared conviction that to the extent their ends coincide with America's, they can be achieved by means more compatible with Contadora interests than the ones Washington has stubbornly employed.

Obviously, the Contadora states are no more eager than the United States to have Soviet power camped on their doorsteps. But they agree with many American critics of the Reagan administration's policy that overthrowing the Sandinistas and decimating the

Salvadoran Left are not needed to prevent that outcome. Their judgment rests on confidence in the will and capability of the United States to deter any Central American government from offering itself as a Soviet base and to deter the Soviet Union from accepting such an improbable offer.

Although their views on how best to promote counterpart regimes in Central America are not entirely uniform, all the Contadora states reject the Reagan scenario, according to which pluralistic regimes will be the residue left by the military defeat of the Sandinistas and the Salvadoran opposition.

Mexico has most explicitly disparaged this scenario and, in fact, sees it as a recipe for promoting extremism. Like many U.S. critics of Reagan administration policy, makers of foreign policy in Mexico believe that military pressure, coupled with political and economic isolation, will strengthen the Sandinista regime's most Leninist elements by helping to justify severe restrictions on a range of democratic freedoms. Even in democracies, civil rights do not prosper in wartime.

But the Contadora countries have more self-interested reasons for rejecting isolation and military pressure, exercised through the Contras, as a policy for dealing with Nicaragua. They fear that the intensified Sandinista repression that could result from an escalation of the U.S.-organized and -armed threat might loosen domestic political restraints on direct United States intervention—the worst possible outcome from the Contadora perspective.

These countries do not seem to envision a Sandinista defeat by any other means. Rather than relying, apparently futilely, no doubt dangerously, on military force, the Contadora regimes would use political and economic means to enlarge the existing obstacles to building a Leninist state: Nicaragua's open and dependent economy; its position squarely in the traditional zone of American influence (which would appear to discourage Soviet-bloc aid beyond levels required to assure the regime's bare survival); its strong Roman Catholic tradition and general cultural orientation toward the

West, especially the United States; and the porosity of its frontiers—there cannot be a Nicaraguan Berlin Wall to prevent the
flight of the skilled and energetic.

Castro exploited just such an exodus to consolidate Marxist
rule in Cuba. The Sandinistas are unlikely to pursue a similar strategy. Indeed, Sandinista leaders regularly concede the failure of the
Cuban economic model and insist on Nicaragua's need for a mixed
economy to fight poverty and achieve development. But the Sandinistas clearly have not even faced, much less resolved, the problem
of how to win private-sector support for their development objectives without giving that sector a significant political role. When
faced with the threat of political emasculation, entrepreneurs in
most countries turn their attentions to the covert export of capital.

Castro solved this problem by fully socializating the economy
and by imposing Draconian controls. These options do not seem
open to Nicaragua's revolutionary elite. In the first place, Castro
survived in part through huge infusions of Soviet aid. At present,
Moscow shows no inclination to provide aid on a comparable scale,
partly because of economic strains and partly because of an accu-
rate appreciation of Nicaragua's marginal strategy value—especially in the light of evident United States will and capacity to
preempt militarily any Soviet effort to establish a strategic military
presence in the country. Precisely because Nicaragua is not part of
the Soviet bloc—not a Marxist state—it cannot invoke the principle
of bloc solidarity. And any effort to satisfy the requisite criteria of
institutional and ideological purity and defense to Soviet leadership
would repel support from democratic socialists and powerfully encourage decisive United States intervention.

In addition, the Sandinistas cannot consolidate support among
a large class of landless laborers by transferring to them a cornucopia of confiscated wealth, as Castro did for his island's sugar-
cane cutters. Nicaragua possesses neither a comparably deprived
class nor a relatively vast infrastructure of affluence. The blacks
and Indians of the Atlantic coast do represent relatively deprived
groups. But because they have always distrusted the Spanish-speak-

ing majority, and because they were generally left alone by the late dictator, Anastasio Somoza Debayle, their attitude toward the revolutionaries varies from indifference to hostility.

Finally, Nicaragua does not possess a single charismatic leader able to rally and sustain mass support for forms of social organization sharply at odds with traditional culture and traditional institutions, above all the Catholic Church.

Although the Contadora colleagues all oppose big-stick diplomacy and favor more pluralistic regimes in Central America, their visions of desirable political systems for the area are no less diverse than their own political orders. Mexico, for example, would feel more comfortable than Colombia and Venezuela with a single dominant party incorporating all important peasant and trade union leaders, controlling the armed forces, and limiting political competitors to the status of a permanent minority. Panama probably would not object to a political order in which the armed forces effectively guaranteed the bounds of political choice.

While the partners probably differ in their conception of the good society, their differences are undoubtedly narrower than superficial comparison of their recent history and formal political institutions would indicate. All the Contadora countries are heirs to the Spanish tradition of centralized power and the Catholic vision of an organic, rather than a Lockeian, contractual society. All are governed by elites little influenced by the egalitarianism of the American and French revolutions. They vary in their assessment of the speed with which emerging social groups should be brought into the power structure. But these differences do not correspond neatly to the degree of formal political competition each regime allows. Thus, the Contadora states have not had to cross great ideological divides to arrive at a common diplomatic front.

The strongest evidence of the priorities of the Contadora states is the basic Central American peace plan they have developed. That the top priority of these countries is not assuring any specific outcome to the conflict, but preventing United States military intervention by containing regional wars, is clear from their continuing emphasis on limiting arms imports and foreign advisors. Their conviction that Honduran support for the Contras is the most likely detonator of regionwide conflict has led the Contadora states continually to strive to end this assistance. In return, they want Nicaragua to refrain from organizing or aiding insurgents and from expanding its military in ways threatening to Honduras.

Isolating the conflict in El Salvador also serves the Contadora interest not only in keeping United States combat forces out of Central America but also in discouraging any sort of foreign involvement tending to convert internal conflicts into international ones. By insisting that the conflict be seen and treated as an essentially domestic struggle rather than as an aspect of U.S.–Soviet relations, the Contadora states hope to isolate the conflict symbolically. And Contadora proposals for what amounts to collective repudiation of aid to all insurgents in the region are especially helpful in symbolically and operationally isolating El Salvador's civil war.

The Contadora commitment to democratization is not merely cosmetic. These countries believe that continuing civil wars will ultimately undermine whatever legal and diplomatic walls they manage to construct. Moreover, in the absence of direct and sustained U.S. intervention, they do not see how Central Americans can achieve domestic and regional harmony—the prerequisites for renewed economic growth—unless each of the embattled Central American states opens its political process.

But the conditions for institutionalizing real pluralism in Guatemala and Nicaragua, if not El Salvador, are hardly auspicious right now. So while the commitments proposed by the Contadora group are serious, they are not functionally integral to the envisioned process of containment. On the contrary, the group views an insistence on the immediate achievement of authentic pluralism as an obstacle to containing the fighting.

## A Historic Crossroads

The Contadora group symbolizes the emergence of politically potent indigenous forces in the Caribbean Basin, forces that, unlike

Cuba, are not beholden to an extrahemispheric power. The group is a symbol precisely because it has managed to become a significant actor. Yet the ultimate significance of its effort remains to be seen. In terms of the kind of raw economic and military power the United States is able to deploy, the Contadora group's assets are trivial. If unreasoning passion and a reckless disregard for costs inspired the Reagan administration to impose a Pax Americana on Central America, the Contadora states could do nothing but bob in the wake of the ensuing disaster. But at this point they retain some capacity to influence Washington, in part by influencing the actions of the Central American states and in part by reiterating to Washington the depth of their collective hostility to United States intention.

Given its theories and passions, the Reagan administration has shown notable restraint in the Central American wars. Fear of a direct confrontation with the Soviet Union and the fall from power of former secretary of state Alexander Haig, Jr., explain much of Washington's loss of interest in directly threatening Cuba, the supposed source of all regional turmoil. But concern about superpower confrontation cannot explain the Reagan administration's failure to send U.S. warplanes into combat over Nicaragua and El Salvador, or to use identifiable American troops to help the Contras establish a ''liberated sector'' in Nicaragua, complete with a provisional government.

The immediate cause of restraint has been congressional and public opinion. But the unusual resistance of Congress and the American public to the Great Communicator's entreaties arguably stems in part from opposition to a more militarized diplomacy voiced by many NATO allies and the Contadora states. The latter may loom larger in U.S. calculations because they are among the dominoes the administration is supposedly protecting—and hence cannot be dismissed with charges of ignorance or gratuitous meddling. Moreover, unlike the West Europeans, the Contadora countries are not constantly indicted as demanding but unappreciative free riders on American power. And because they are, in general, very ably represented in Washington and because on several occasions they have had access to high officials, including the president, Contadora leaders may also have sowed some doubts within the administration itself about the prudence of its preferences.

In addition, the formation of a united front has unquestionably affected United States policy in Central America by reinforcing each Contadora country's confidence in its preferred policies and by influencing the political environment in Central America itself. Without mutual reinforcement and the political safety found in numbers, the individual Contadora states would have had more difficulty resisting administration pressure to adopt its view of the crisis in Central America and its solution. Had two or three of the Contadora states succumbed and the holdout been silenced, leaving Washington free to define reality and extinguish any sense of alternatives, Central American enthusiasts for military solutions in the region—such as Alvarez—would have found themselves in psychologically and politically more commanding positions.

The United States can negotiate the neutralization of Nicaragua. Accepting neutralization would not mean abandoning Nicaragua to unchecked authoritarian rule. While the United States would agree to end military harrassment, it would continue to treat the country as a pariah, denying the economic assistance and access to American markets necessary to transform Nicaragua into a prosperous polity—until the leadership moved toward objectives announced in the neutralization agreements. And in case of a serious deterioration of human rights, the United States could renew aid to the rebels who would then inevitably reemerge.

America should not underestimate either our material or symbolic assets. A United States ready to lavish aid on a politically plural Nicaragua (even if the Sandinistas rule in the moderately authoritarian style of Mexico's PRI) will exert profound influence on the Nicaraguan political system.

As it blunders after military solutions without counting the cost to the people of Central America, the Reagan administration unintentionally demonstrates the difference between a ruthless and a wise diplomacy.

# CHAPTER 2

# International Law and Other Delusions

### ERNEST VAN DEN HAAG

---

## International Law and Nicaragua

*International Law.* Tom Farer has been for many years professor of international law at Rutgers University and elsewhere. It seems only natural that he sincerely believes that international law (1) exists, (2) should play an important role in foreign policy, and (3) is a useful guide for policy toward the civil war in Nicaragua and El Salvador. But he is wrong on all three counts.

Professor Farer may offer his own activities—and those of other international lawyers—as proof of the existence of international law. Yet there are professors of theology, priests, ministers, and many faithful believers, and their activities do not prove that God exists, is influential, or is a useful guide to our actions on this earth. The existence of theologians merely shows that people believe in God—not that he exists. And international lawyers show that people believe in international law, and that the belief helps keep them busy—not that international law exists.

Professor Farer's activities do not convince me that international law is more than some rather incoherent ideas, nor do his arguments persuade me that international law would be useful if it did exist. On the contrary, I believe that the illusion of international law, so diligently pursued by Farer, and bodies such as the U.N., is pernicious and misleading. Anyone who takes it seriously in my opinion disqualifies himself from being taken seriously in discussions of foreign policy.

What I have said so starkly will shock some readers. My fellow Americans believe in the rule of law. So do I. We also believe in the ability of law to settle conflicts peacefully, and to do justice (at least more justice than would be done without law) in the United States and in other domestic jurisdictions. This belief of ours—which I think can readily be supported by the historical and contemporary facts—tends to mislead many of us into believing that what holds true for the domestic order ought to be true (and some even think is true) for international relations as well. They too ought to be (or, some believe, they are) regulated and limited by law. Professor Farer appears to share this delusion. I don't.

Why is international law a delusion? Why can it never be more? Let me start at the beginning. Nation-states,* such as France, the United States, Cuba, the Soviet Union, China, or Nicaragua, are sovereign. Sovereignty was defined by Jean Bodin, one of Professor Farer's more illustrious predecessors, in the 17th century as *potestas legibus absoluta:* power unfettered by (independent of) law. A sovereign nation through its constitutional or *de facto* authorities—monarchs, parliaments, courts—is the supreme lawgiver for its territory. There can be no lawgiver, or law, superior to its own lawgiving authority—else it would not be supreme—or to its own law, if the nation is sovereign. To repeat, there can be no law superior to, and regulative of, the laws a sovereign nation gives itself, no law except its own, to regulate its behavior toward others.

I hasten to add that nations make treaties and accept international obligations, either bilaterally or multilaterally (e.g., the U.N.

---

*"Nation" and "state" are different concepts, the former a social, the latter a political and legal one. Thus, the Soviet Union is actually a multinational state. But the difference is irrelevant for my present purpose and I have used the words as synonyms.

charter is a multilateral treaty). And they follow customs that, whether or not stipulated in documents, are regarded as binding (e.g., the extraterritoriality of embassies, the immunity of accredited diplomats, the willingness to pay debts or to settle conflicts among citizens of different nations according to accepted rules). But all these obligations are voluntarily assumed and will be carried out only as long as the sovereign nation that assumed them is inclined to carry them out. That nation—and that nation alone—decides whether to fulfill obligations, interpret them away, or ignore them. Whereas domestic law provides for enforcement of obligations, "international law" does not, and cannot, because nations, unlike citizens, are not subjected to laws other than those they are willing to accept at any given time. Thus, nothing is actually binding in "international law," let alone enforceable, and nothing, therefore, is law.

Usually a nation will not contract obligations unless it wishes, or finds its convenient, to fulfill them, particularly since other nations may retaliate if it does not. But circumstances change, and if a nation does not fulfill its obligations as seen by other nations, the latter have ultimately no way of forcing it, other than going to war. Thus, nations may repudiate foreign debts. (They do so rarely because it harms their credit standing. But occasionally they do, and there is no effective legal remedy—no bankruptcy administrator.) Or nations may act contrary to treaty obligations. Or use violence against other nations, i.e., go to war. All that other nations can do is defend themselves and to win, if they are strong enough. International law cannot help. Only power does. Power—*potestas legibus absoluta*—independent of law.

Even the most universally accepted and mutually convenient obligations are not always adhered to, and there is no way of enforcing them by legal means. Iran found it convenient—largely for domestic political reasons—to disregard diplomatic privileges honored for many centuries by sovereign nations. Our embassy was occupied and our diplomats were taken prisoner and maltreated. We could do nothing except use force to free them. We did nothing. Finally, Iran, after many months, decided to free our diplomats in exchange for financial rewards. There was no way to enforce "international law," let alone to punish the Iranian government.

During World War II the allies, on the brink of victory, decided to punish the German leaders for "waging aggressive war." They did so after defeating the Nazis. They based their proceedings, which took place in Nuremberg, on the (thinly veiled) *ex post facto* law they had fashioned. (German leaders were also charged with violating laws that had existed when they violated them, but that is a different matter.) The allies contravened (as only the Nazis and the Soviets had done before in modern times) the Roman principle *nullum crimen sine lege* (there is no crime without a [preexisting] law) and *nulla poena sine lege* (there is no legal punishment without [preexisting] law) by executing the German leaders after (an otherwise fair) trial. These leaders deserved no less morally.

But the court that sentenced the Nazis included Soviet judges, although the Soviet Union itself had attacked Finland before being attacked by Germany. The Soviet attack on Finland was no less an act of aggression than the German attack on Poland. It was so labeled by the allies. There was no "international law" providing for trying the Soviet leaders. Their domestic cruelty against Russians and minorities was barely second to that of the Germans. But they were not tried.

Anyway, the precedent set at Nuremberg did not hold. Despite "international law" there have been more than a hundred wars since World War II. To mention a few: India–Pakistan, Israel–Egypt, Iran–Iraq (still going on at this writing), and many others. There have been many invasions too. The Soviet Union invaded Czechoslovakia, and also Hungary, to institute governments it preferred. Lately it has invaded Afghanistan, where its troops are still fighting. Turkey invaded Cyprus. Lybia invaded Chad. In none of these wars or invasions has anyone been charged with aggression.

No one has been tried or sentenced. The Nuremburg trials set no precedent.

A law must be something more than just a moral norm. It must issue from a legislative authority and be enforceable by courts. I am not suggesting that a law that is not always enforced is not a law. We do have laws against burglary and we do have burglary. But with respect to burglary (and other domestic laws, civil and criminal), the injured party, or the prosecutor, can invoke a law and compel the suspect to appear in court and, if found guilty, to suffer punishment or to pay compensation. The court can compel the acceptance of its decision and compliance with its directives as well as the payment of whatever is owed.

Not so with international law. Even if nations say that they will accept the jurisdiction of an international tribunal, they reserve to themselves the right to decide whether they actually will in any case. And if the international court finds against them they can, if they want, ignore its verdicts. Nations need not even be powerful to do so. Albania has simply ignored judgments of the International Court of Justice, according to which it owes money to Great Britain—which could collect only by making war. In domestic law the courts have compulsory jurisdiction and can count on a coercive apparatus superior to that of any subject: police and military forces. In international law there is no compulsory jurisdiction (which would be inconsistent with sovereignty), and the coercive power of every nation is superior to that of the court, since the court has none. (It could scarcely have power superior to that of, say, the Soviet Union, or the United States.)

What Professor Farer insists on calling "international law" is thus but a series of rules, principles, customs, treaties, and agreements, which are adhered to when the sovereign nations find it convenient to follow them, and disregarded when it is convenient to do so. This is why the danger of war is ever present, and why international relations are based on power, not, as Mr. Farer thinks, on law. Law, at most, is used cosmetically. Indeed, the U.N. is simply a name for all the member nations together, at best an international organization. Only a supernational one could effectively order any nation to do anything. International law merely obscures the fact that foreign policy—be it that of Afghanistan, China, the United States, the Soviet Union, or Great Britain— has to do with power, not with law. The purpose is to secure enough power to be safe from attack, or to expand.

Is there a better way? I doubt it. I cannot see a tribunal effectively deciding serious conflicts between the United States and the Soviet Union, and enforcing its judgments. Neither power would give up its sovereignty—its right to defend its interests as it sees fit—to such a tribunal. Neither would disarm so that the tribunal could impose its verdict. At best we may occasionally have international arbitration of minor cases voluntarily submitted. But for this we hardly need the International Court of Justice or international law.

*P.S.* For aficionados of legal argument, I should note that Professor Farer is (almost) right on one point. When Nicaragua complained to the International Court of Justice we should simply have responded that the United States does not recognize the competence of the court to hear this case and therefore will not appear in response to the complaint.

However, our state department lawyers thought our case against the competence of the court in the dispute was so good (it was) that they could not restrain themselves from arguing it. So they argued to attempt to persuade the court that it lacked jurisdiction. They failed. Thereupon they decided not to defend the case further in court after all. But once you argue a case before a tribunal, you imply recognition of its competence to decide it, including deciding its own competence. Hence, our behavior was foolish. (Not that it matters.)

Our behavior was doubly foolish since it is obvious that, regardless of the nature of the case, the International Court of Justice (whose members are elected by the U.N.) will decide any conflict between the United States and an undeveloped country in favor of the latter. Thus, we might as well save ourselves the effort. Indeed, it is foolish of us to submit *any* cases to the International Court of Justice—even if it is likely to decide them reasonably as it did, for example, in the U.S.–Canadian fisheries dispute. To submit such disputes to this court only enhances its prestige, which ultimately will be used for anti-American purposes. Anything this court decides could as well be decided by an *ad hoc* arbitration board. So why should the United States support the illusion of Professor Farer and his friends—why should we act as though there is an impartial international tribunal to which serious disputes could be submitted with the expectation that verdicts will be carried out by non-Western powers?

*Nicaragua.* What has all this to do with our policy in Central America, and specifically Nicaragua? Before seriously analyzing the problem we have to remove Mr. Farer's odd idea that "international law" could shape policies or determine the behavior of Nicaraguans or their friends and enemies. Our policy in Nicaragua must be based on what we stand to lose and gain there, the costs we may incur, the risks we can assume and avoid, and the benefits we can expect.

Consider the situation. Nicaragua had long been governed by dictators. Somoza *père* installed himself with the help of departing American marines. When he died he left the country, so to speak, to Somoza *fils*, who ran it for his own benefit, stealing as much as possible (a great deal) and treating his opponents in the time-honored Central American way, i.e., killing them whenever he found it useful. Somoza was an old-style dictator. He ran the government of Nicaragua and brooked no competition. But there remained fairly independent power centers, such as the Roman Catholic Church, the business community, and even independent and uncensored opposition papers. Somoza pretty much left alone those who did not bother or endanger him, e.g., the Miskito Indian minority. He provided stability even if at the high cost of dictatorship, inefficiency, and corruption. He also was pro-American.

Somoza always had enemies. Originally these enemies, led by Augusto Sandino, had waged a guerrilla war against the occupation by American marines. Later they fought against the Somozas. By the time Jimmy Carter became president of the United States the guerrillas had had some modest and temporary successes. They presented no serious danger to the dictatorship. However, through a series of insensate policies Somoza *fils* alienated the church—which anyway was beginning to object to rightist dictatorships in Latin countries—and the business community. He relied on the National Guard, a privileged, well-armed body, the only military organization in Nicaragua. But his enemies gained political if not military strength. Jimmy Carter finally withdrew American support and told Somoza to abdicate. This meant no arms for the National Guard, no financial support, and, most important, a signal for all of Somoza's enemies, that, with an appropriate effort, they could win, and enjoy the fruits of victory undisturbed, without American political or military interference. They proceeded to do so.

At first the Sandinistas included in their government all the forces that had helped defeat Somoza (who had fled to Paraguay, where he was murdered by terrorists). The government promised civil liberties and the institution of a democracy. We subsidized it and offered assistance. But within a short time it became clear to most observers—though not to Professor Farer—that the hard core of Sandinista comandantes were Communists and intended to institute the usual Communist type of government. They proceeded inexorably, as fast, or as slowly as circumstances permitted and with the prescribed zig zags. The democratic elements left the government or were ousted. The most exposed ones left the country. Private enterprise was stifled. Opposition papers were censored. A Sandinista Roman Catholic Church independent of the bishops and the Vatican was promoted. Military forces were steadily increased with the help of Cuban and Eastern European instructors. Support was sought and received from Moscow (mainly through Eastern Europe). In turn, arms and support were given to the Communist or proto-Communist guerrillas fighting against the Socialist Duarte regime in El Salvador, which the United States supported.

With the election of Ronald Reagan the United States faced the reality of Nicaragua. We ceased to try to appease the comandantes, although it took us quite a while to stop lending money or importing bananas. We started to organize a motley array of anti-Sandinista forces called Contras. Based largely in Honduras, and armed by the United States, these forces are trying to prevent the institution of a totalitarian Communist regime in Nicaragua. They have not been successful so far, but they may be slowing the process.

The Left in the United States did not and does not like our support of the Contras. Neither do the erstwhile supporters of Jimmy Carter. They contend that, yes, there are some Communists in Nicaragua, but, no, the government is not Communist (What is it? They do not say), and if, instead of supporting the Contras, we would just be nice to the comandantes and go on subsidizing them, we could wean them away from their pro-Soviet, anti-American stance and help them become democratic Socialists or whatever. This view has been shared by such European Socialists as Willi Brandt, a leader of the German Socialists and former German chancellor, and by Olaf Palme, the leader of the Swedish Socialists, and prime minister, until murdered recently (by an assailant unknown at this writing).

The appeasement view favored by Professor Farer was also proposed in regard to Cuba, where we originally welcomed the revolution too and were told every day by *The New York Times* and by all liberals that fundamentally the revolution could be steered into a democratic direction if we just were nice to Mr. Castro. We tried. Fidel Castro, however, in an unusual attack of candor, disappointed his American followers by simply saying one day that he had always been a Communist and had no desire to swerve from the Communist course, whatever the Americans did. Cuba has since become a Communist dictatorship neither better nor worse than, say, Romania. It has also become a Soviet satellite and a supporter of Communist guerrillas willing to follow the party line.

Professor Farer is unable to learn from the experience, and he tells us about Nicaragua what his friends (I don't remember whether he himself did) told us about Cuba: We can wean the Nicaraguan Communists away from following the Soviet line by being nice to them. (The most inveterate liberals actually tell us the same about the Soviet Union itself. Had we been nicer they would never have become Communists, and if we are nicer they will become Democrats.) Other American recurrences about Nicaragua are notable. Numerous groups, often under church auspices, go to visit the country and come back estatic—just as they used to come back from Stalin's Soviet Union, Mao's China, Castro's Cuba, etc. Despite the fact that the Nicaraguan government persecutes churches as much as it dares (the population is faithful to the churches), American clerics of all denominations extol the Nicaraguan government. (Well, what else is new?)

We have three options about Nicaragua: (1) Invade and conquer. (2) Support the Contras. (3) Do nothing, or negotiate with the Nicaraguan government, which assumes that we can get and can trust promises of good behavior in exchange for American support—good behavior meaning (a) reduction of Nicaraguan armed forces, (b) nonalignment, (c) democratization, "human rights," free elections with opposition participation, and civil rights for all.

1. We could easily occupy all major Nicaraguan centers. This could have the advantage of eliminating the Nicaraguan military forces, which constitute a threat to Central America; of eliminating effective support by Nicaragua of antigovernment guerrillas elsewhere in Central America, e.g., El Salvador; and of preventing establishment of any Soviet bases, political or military, in Nicaragua.

The conquest of the main military centers in Nicaragua would be easy. However, an endemic guerrilla war in the countryside would be practically guaranteed. Even if the Sandinistas had few followers left, anti-Yanqui sentiment is strong for historical reasons. America doesn't have the stomach for an endless guerrilla war, even if the occupation of Nicaragua were clearly in the American interest. The Sandinistas could count on no less sympathy in the United States than was available to the Vietnamese Communists. Consequently, Americans would, in all likelihood, give up sometime during the guerrilla war, leaving the pro-American faction in Nicaragua to the tender mercies of the Communists. Hence, this option should be rejected.

2. Fortunately there is no compelling American interest to drive us to invade Nicaragua. By supporting the Contras we can be sure to distract and weaken the Nicaraguan government enough to prevent it from being a threat to its neighbors. Moreover, our support for the Contras makes it entirely clear that we would support these neighbors against any Nicaraguan attempt to overwhelm them. Our support is also a clear signal to the Soviets—if one were needed—that we will not tolerate major Soviet bases in Central America. All this for perhaps $100 million per year—less than we have given annually to kleptocratic clowns such as Samuel Doe in Liberia or Baby Doc Duvalier in Haiti.

Finally, our support of the Contras may become enough of a threat to the comandantes in time to lead them to make concessions to democracy. They will do so only if forced. They may fear to be overthrown. Or the defense against the Contras may become too expensive and disorganizing for them. Not least, our support of the Contras will suggest limits of expansion to Cuba and the Soviet Union. Moreover, the latter will have either to pay for the extravagances and the military power of the comandantes (as we did in part for Somoza) or to face their fall from power. We need not worry about their dilemma, but we should do our best to accentuate it.

What we need to worry about is whether our domestic opposition (such as Professor Farer's) to a rational foreign policy will be strong enough to prevent us from carrying it out effectively. I hope not.

3. Professor Farer's solution is to follow "international law"

and to appease the comandantes, to exact promises and to believe them, without compelling the comandantes or reducing their power. He has presented his arguments for his position and I need not summarize them.

I have tried to refute his illusions about international law and about appeasing the Nicaraguan Communists as well as I can. Readers will have to draw their own conclusions.

II

CHAPTER 3

# Why I Remain Unpersuaded

## TOM J. FARER

Professor van den Haag has clearly been moved by Voltaire's dictum: "When fact and reason fail, turn to ridicule." The tactic can be effective except where, as in this instance, ridicule is dragged to such extreme lengths that it becomes ridiculous.

The good professor has opened his contribution to our debate by both parodying my views and misunderstanding law. This is good, and not only for my polemical purposes, but because it returns us to basic issues that are generally overlooked in discourse about foreign policy. One of those issues is, of course, the nature and utility of international law.

Many lawyers, in addition to laymen of all sorts, concur with Professor van den Haag's notion that international law is an illusion nurtured by a handful of self-serving acolytes, an illusion that is, moreover, pernicious to the extent that it influences American foreign policy. This notion stems from a particular conception of law—namely, as a cluster of rules declared, imposed, and enforced by governments; in other words, as orders backed by threats. Because in our daily experience law is associated with police and courts, a tendency to equate the two is quite natural. A hundred years ago even fairly reflective people generally accepted this equation. For contemporary legal scholars, however, it is simply a relic, rejected because it provides an inadequate explanation of how people use and why they obey the law.

Obviously nothing will be gained by initiating a battle of definitions wherein Professor van den Haag and I claim that by means of intuition, divine inspiration, or some process of logical derivation we have respectively discovered the true meaning of the word *law*.Words have no true meaning. Like Humpty Dumpty, we are free to ascribe to them any meaning at all.

In effect, Professor van den Haag has launched just such a futile struggle by claiming that international law does not exist. He concedes that the international scene is littered with materials— e.g., treaties, charters, customs "regarded as binding"—that imply the presence of law both because they look like the materials employed in national legal systems and because they create "obligations." But, he hastens to claim, we nevertheless do not have law because "these obligations are voluntarily assumed, and will be carried out only as long as the sovereign nation that assumed them is inclined to carry them out." The crux of the matter, for him, is that "Whereas domestic law provides for enforcement of obligations, 'international law' does not, and cannot, because nations, unlike citizens, are not subjected to laws other than those they are willing to accept at any given time. Thus, nothing is actually binding in 'international law,' let alone enforceable, and nothing therefore is law."

Since in ordinary usage the word *obligation* is virtually synonymous with being bound ("something that one is bound to do," definition 3 in *Webster's New Collegiate Dictionary,* Merriam, 1973, p. 792), I can make sense of the quoted language only if I restate it as follows: "I choose to believe that law exists only where obligations, however they may arise, are interpreted and enforced by an authority independent of and both formally and practically superior to the obligated party."

Professor van den Haag's effort to define international law out of existence is an exercise in irrelevance. It is also arrestingly incongruous. For while the professor advertises himself as an austere realist, his mode of argument and the issue he purports to address — whether international law exists — heralds the presence of some dreamy metaphysician. A practical person concerned with policy matters is not likely to worry overmuch about the existence or non-existence of some sort of Platonic essence called ''international law.'' What he or she should want to know is whether treaties and customs deemed obligatory exercise an independent influence on the behavior of states and/or whether, to paraphrase that great realist Oliver Wendell Holmes, they are important aids in predicting how states are likely to behave.

These are, thank goodness, factual not metaphysical inquiries that can be carried out by conventional methods for gathering information and can, at least in theory, lead to a conclusion that is not predetermined by dogma. If, as a matter of fact, treaties and custom do influence the behavior of governments, then reasonably prudent people will want to take them into account in formulating policy. They might not be decisive, but surely they would be relevant.

Empirical inquiries invariably begin with the formulation of a hypothesis. The hypothesis is a provisional statement about the world that, in light of the results of prior inquiries into related matters or common experience, seems more likely than not to be true. I take it that Professor van den Haag believes we should begin by assuming that there is nothing in the relations among states closely approximating, much less essentially identical to, the ''law'' to be found within states that works both to promote collective interests by defining the limits of individual choice (principally in the form of criminal law and a multitude of regulatory statutes enforced by civil penalties) and to facilitate cooperation among individuals by stabilizing their agreements (primarily through the law of contracts). I will now suggest why the reverse hypothesis is a much more plausible point of departure.

Writers about international relations have often referred to the ''community of nations.'' The word *community* is apt because it connotes intimate and structured and enduring relations among a group of actors. The relations among states have just these characteristics. In number fewer than 200, even including such giants as the Cook Islands and Lichtenstein, they compare with one of the smaller villages in my home state of New Hampshire. Although thousands of miles separate many members of the international community, like the inhabitants of a village they interact constantly and, because of the division of labor that emerges over time in any stable group, as well as the inevitable efficiencies associated with cooperation, they have acquired an impressive measure of interdependence.

In any case where we see a group whose members interact constantly, much less one marked by a high degree of interdependence, by extrapolating from our personal experience of small-group relations or the historical development of customary law within states we can reasonably assume that the character of their interactions are, by and large, predictable. For under those circumstances, random and unpredictable behavior would be inefficient and costly. Moreover, the very existence of interdependence implies the priority of long-term cooperative relations: If each member made his own weapons, consumed only the food he grew, and relied entirely on himself and his family for self-defense, interdependence would not have arisen in the first place.

Relatively stable, complementary relations between governors and those they govern can, of course, be voluntary or coerced. (Our personal experience suggests they are very likely to be a mixture of both.) Even if totally coerced in the sense that raw force alone prevents most of the inhabitants of the state from altering their behavior, both the elites who control the government and third parties dealing with that government will regard various directives to the population as law in the sense that the subjects are seen to have an obligation to obey and appear likely to obey. Even in the case of what begins as a purely coercive relationship, positive forms of reciprocity are almost certain to emerge over time. In the first place, governments invariably want their subjects to perform various functions: pay taxes, construct public works, repair roads, grow crops for market, serve in the armed forces. To achieve these ends, the government must itself act in a predictable way—for example, in meting out punishment. Occasionally it may punish arbitrarily as part of a conscious policy of terrorizing the subject population. But the frequent application of punishment for acts or omissions that at the time of their commission were consistent with prevailing orders disorients as it terrorizes. In the process it removes a powerful incentive for compliance. For if a subject is almost as likely to be punished for docile compliance as for resistance, resistance will grow.

Although governments may therefore impose consistency on themselves purely as an act of self-interest, over time the subject population will tend to form a set of expectations about governmental behavior that gradually evolve from simple predictions of how the authorities will act in certain circumstances to how they "ought" to act. Expectations of continuity may simply be inherent in human nature. As these expectations harden, deviations come increasingly to be seen as infuriatingly arbitrary surprises.

Students of popular revolts have noted that they are most likely to occur not during long eras of unrelieved mass misery but rather when, after a period of improved conditions have raised expectations, those expectations are frustrated by signs of regression.

Prudent rulers will therefore attempt to explain and justify change and to do so in ways most appealing to their audience—that is, by emphasizing or at least invoking a general interest in the particular change. Since their attempts at justification will imply normative limits to the legislative process (i.e., the process of promulgating and applying generally applicable orders), the subject population and even its governors will find themselves increasingly infused with a sense that the legislative process defines the obligations of the legislators as well as the subjects of legislation or, more succinctly, that everyone is a subject of "the law."

Actually, prudent rulers will attempt at an early point in their dominion to promote a sense of reciprocal obligation and interest

because government by raw power is both expensive and inefficient. Wherever rulers cannot acquire an aura of legitimacy by
claiming convincingly to be the agents of a deity worshipped by
their subjects, they can build legitimacy and its concomitant, uncoerced obedience, only by demonstrating links between the secular
interests of governed and governors. Most ruling elites can at a
minimum invoke a joint interest in defending the national territory
against external forces. In the Middle Ages, feudal lords used the
rationale of collective self-defense to justify dominion over their
serfs. Normally, there will also be a plausible shared interest in
maintaining law and order against the threat of common criminality
and in promoting economic growth.

So although a governing elite may have initially installed itself
by means of thumbscrews and gallows, if it successfully deters or
repels aggression, establishes domestic tranquillity, administers an
economy of growing affluence, and behaves predictably, then, assuming it also has the good sense to admit men and women of talent
from nonelite families, it will acquire an aura of legitimacy; in other
words, most citizens will begin to obey elite commands not out of
fear but rather out of a sense of obligation to respect the law.

Once this occurs, not only do the costs of domination radically
diminish, in addition, the rulers can tap all the synergistic potential
of a community where mutual interest, if not a fully developed
sense of community, has replaced fear as the principal ordering
device of politics and society.

After acquiring legitimacy, rulers find that one of the most
effective means for maintaining it is by establishing formal equality
for all citizens within the legal system. If, for example, they wish to
prevent the poor from sleeping under bridges, then, as Anatole
France mordantly noted, they can achieve that objective without
formal discrimination by a general prohibition. At least in theory,
no one is exempt, not even the wealthy inebriate.

The puissance of forms will fail, however, if their substance is
regularly gutted by improvised exceptions. Thus, while the elite

may retain the raw power to exploit every transient advantage in defiance of the law and although in light of that power one can say that, unlike the mass of the population, the elite class "voluntarily assumed" the obligation of law compliance, appreciation of its long-term interests will inhibit *ad hoc* deviations from the law in order to seize some minor advantage. The strongest states in international society hold a position in relation to the mass of weak states that corresponds closely to the position of governing elites in relation to the rest of the citizens of national societies.

As I noted earlier, because it is inhabited by a relative handful of actors in a condition of intense interaction and interdependence, the international system can easily be analogized to a village. Within villages, the common interest in increasing productivity by means of specialization encourages economic exchange. The exchange economy will not develop, however, unless families can rely on each other's promises. Who, for instance, would be foolish enough to specialize in weaving blankets rather than growing crops unless they could rely on promises from a farming family to exchange a certain amount of food for each blanket?

In the village, as in the international system, some families may be more numerous, better armed, or otherwise more capable of coercion than others. But for the reasons I suggested above, reliance on raw power is almost certain to result in failure to realize the village's full economic potential. Moreover, weaker families will be prompted to band together against the bullies or to ally themselves with strong families who agree to be less abusive or simply to play one bully off against the other. It is not hard, therefore, to see why even the powerful should be inclined to abide by custom and formal agreement irrespective of the existence of courts and police.

Courts and police are reflexively treated as intrinsic to a legal system because most people extrapolate from the huge, anonymous metropolitan societies in which they live, societies where the vast majority of transactions are between strangers (for example, the mugger and his victim, or a pharmaceutical company and its millions of customers) and where the provenance of an injury is often obscure. (Did the building collapse because of bad design, a failure of performance by one of twenty subcontractors, a defect in the steel produced by a subsidiary of a holding company with a million or so shareholders?) To repeat, the international community is far closer in its essential characteristics to the isolated village than to some vast sprawling urban complex. The inhabitants, states, are few and with rare exceptions permanent. Their actions and the consequences of those actions are hard to conceal. Mutually beneficial cooperation requires a fair degree of confidence that each member of the community will comply with established custom and with promises.

Compliance irrespective of the existence of courts and police is actually more likely to occur in the international system than in towns and villages, much less cities and whole countries. One reason is that bureaucracies normally institutionalize assessment of longer-term interests: They are generally more methodical in this respect than individuals standing alone. Moreover, being populated by individuals with their cross-cutting ambitions and interests, bureaucracies are slower to react, less capable, and less inclined to pursue instant gratification.

The second and more important reason is, ironically, one of those cited by Professor van den Haag to prove that international law does not exist—namely, the fact that its obligations are voluntarily assumed. Within nations, laws that limit the range of permissible behavior often reflect the preferences of some part of the population rather than the general will. Those who opposed passage of the law experience it as an imposition. Out of fear of punishment or a sense of obligation to law in general, they may nevertheless obey. But these motives for compliance are not reenforced, as would be true in the case of those who supported the law's adoption, by a sense of acting to fulfill one's self-interest or personal values.

The international community has no centralized law-making institution. Its "laws" arise either out of explicit agreements among states or out of universal acceptance of certain customary behavior as obligatory; the latter source of law could be described as "implied agreements." As I wrote in my opening argument: "Precisely because international law reflects the will of all the parties it governs, rather than being a body of norms imposed often against the will of some portion of the affected actors, it *must* embody shared moral values and strategic interests."

I then went on to argue that the United States, as the richest, most powerful, and most influential state, in classical strategic parlance as a *status quo* power, has a particular interest in reinforcing the international legal system, since that system expresses and helps to maintain the existing order of things.

To be sure, as Professor van den Haag points out, "circumstances change." The change may be nothing more than a transient shift in the balance of interests or power, or it may be something more profound. If it is the former, governments must consider whether the short-term gains to be harvested from noncompliance with governing norms outweigh the costs. The costs are threefold. One is retaliation, a danger the professor himself underscores, though without appreciating its significance to a decentralized legal system. States, like individuals under national legal systems, enjoy a wide range of discretion within which acts designed, however selfishly, to promote their interests are deemed legitimate. Adversely affected parties may respond, but not as a matter of principle. But where a state evades reciprocal obligations, it invites retaliation as a matter of principle. Thus, it may experience a hostile response from states not materially affected, and the response of those materially affected may exceed their material injury.

In a legal system marked by obligations voluntarily assumed on the basis of mutuality of interest, deviance invites deviance. Thus, a second prospective cost of delinquency is a general reduction in the level of compliance with the violated norm. A third prospective cost is some overall shrinkage of confidence in the system itself. A slump in expectations of compliance encourages short-term calculations of interest and correspondingly obstructs efforts to stabilize behavior in areas where the potential delinquent would benefit from enhanced cooperation.

Professor van den Haag and others who claim that international law is somehow not real law evince a curious obsession with punishment narrowly conceived as the imposition of criminal sanctions. They presume that law functions only in the shadow of the prison and the gallows. Where those props are unavailable, so-called realists impose on those claiming that law exists an insuperable burden of proof—namely, that there is universal compliance with standards of behavior deemed obligatory.

Conversely—as is made clear by Professor van den Haag's brief reference to the incidence of burglary—when obligations are backed by the full majesty of courts with compulsory jurisdiction, police, and prisons, irrespective of their efficacy he and his fellow believers will find law. I have no interest in investigating the psychological sources of this fetishistic emphasis on the apparatus of criminal punishment. My concern is with its consequences, above all with the resulting inability to imagine the strength of other sorts of sanctions or to see the limitations of the criminal law model.

Astute as he is, Professor van den Haag is not blind to the existence of such sanctions as (1) refusal to deal with parties who arbitrarily repudiate their obligations and (2) responsive repudiation. In the world of business, these sanctions may well be more effective than the threat of litigation in enforcing compliance with contractual obligations. The relations among the independent, formally equal states of the international system are also analogous to the relations among businesses with competitive but at the same time complementary interests. Hence, a contract-law model is superior to the criminal-law model as a means for understanding how obligations arise and survive slight shifts in the balance of advantage associated with any particular deal.

The short of the matter is that both the study of legal systems and the analysis of national interest strongly support my hypothesis that the system of reciprocal obligation normally referred to as "international law" does influence the behavior of states. The hypothesis also draws powerful support from empirical data. The structure and functioning of foreign policy bureaucracies cannot be satisfactorily explained in any other way. If the obligations assumed by adhering to treaties or conceding claims about the binding character of custom were deemed susceptible to almost cost-free abandonment, the care with which governments approach these activities would be inexplicable. In the area of arms control, for example, the Soviets no less than we exhibit exquisite concern over every linguistic nuance, including conditions for suspending or terminating the obligations assumed.

Equally suggestive are the policy options that never reach the decision-making agenda. As the distinguished political scientist Robert Tucker pointed out at the time of the Arab oil boycott and first price escalation, prior to the Second World War the disparity in military power between the West and the OPEC countries would have discouraged the latter's initiative. In an era when force was still regarded as a legitimate instrument for protecting important national interests, powerful countries would simply not have tolerated such a costly blow to their economies.

Both the horror and the ideological polarities of World War II gave preeminence to a long-accumulating sentiment in favor of abolition of military force except as an instrument of self-defense against actual or imminent attack. Abolitionists codified their triumph in the United Nations Charter and the judgment of the Nuremberg Tribunal condemning wars of aggression and subjecting claims of self-defense to objective appraisal. In 1956 the United States helped reaffirm the prohibition of force by orchestrating United Nations condemnation of the Anglo-French attempt to reoccupy the Suez Canal Zone and by forcing withdrawal of the expeditionary force. Seventeen years later the antiforce norm was still potent enough to marginalize those few voices urging the United States to threaten military action in the Persian Gulf. Anyone who has actually worked, as I have, within the foreign policy bureaucracy can cite many other cases where actions plainly prohibited by international treaty or custom, yet arguably cost-effective on other grounds, have failed to surface at high policy-making levels.

After reconsidering the matter, Professor van den Haag will concede, I trust, that a sense of obligation arising from international treaty and custom does influence the behavior of states.

His silence would seem to imply the further concession that our extensive and continuing assistance to the Contras—including training, arming, advising, and direct collaboration in military operations, for example, by providing data on the location and movement of Nicaraguan troops—violates our treaty commitments under the United Nations Charter and the Organization of American States, as well as our obligations under customary international law. Such a concession is appropriate in light of the argument I developed in Chapter 1 and also of the subsequent decision of the International Court of Justice issued on June 27, 1986.

By a vote of 12 to 3 the Court found that United States involvement with the Contras violated universally recognized standards governing the use of force and respect for national sovereignty. Professor van den Haag's anticipatory disparagement of the Court is as cavalier as it is indifferent to fact. His claim, for instance, that the Court "will decide any conflict between the United States and an underdeveloped country in favor of the latter" is flatly contradicted by the Court's 1979 decision finding the Iranian government to have violated international law by failing to end the seizure of our embassy in Teheran and the detention of its occupants.

That judges of the Court are elected by the General Assembly of the United Nations does not constitute persuasive proof of an anti-American bias. The professor conveniently overlooks the actual composition of the Court. One of the judges is a United States citizen. Five others are citizens of United States allies: France,

Italy, Norway, Japan, and Britain. The Brazilian and Argentine judges are from states linked to the United States through the Rio Treaty (our Western Hemisphere equivalent of NATO) and whose successive governments have varied in their ideological complexion from centrist to rightist. Of the two African judges, one is from Senegal, a country intimately associated with and dependent on France and a consistent friend of the West in African forums. The other is from Nigeria, a country that has regularly distanced itself from third world radicals. Nor are the judges from China and India likely to be knee-jerk opponents of U.S. interests, assuming, as I do, that judges will generally reflect the orientation of their home states. (The assumption is reasonable on a number of grounds, not least among them being the unwritten rule at the United Nations that candidates for the Court must be nominated by their home states.) Under analysis, then, the Court emerges as a body more likely than not to register the legal values and perspectives of the West.

Given all that Professor van den Haag must concede insofar as law is concerned, if he is to take a stand at all it must be on the ground that the interests the United States has at stake in Central America justify our incurring the costs of delinquency. In order to maintain that position, he must demonstrate not only that the stakes are at least substantial but also that their loss is likely if we comply fully with the law. In opening the second section of his initial response, he frames the governing issues in very similar terms: "Our policy in Nicaragua must be based on what we stand to lose and gain there, the costs we may incur, the risks we can assume and avoid, and the benefits we can expect." As a guide for policy appraisal this is impeccable, but so malleable that it can be wrapped cosmetically around any conceivable policy.

## The Calculus of U.S. Interests

When my colleague in this dialectical adventure turns from law to policy, he evidently stands on firmer and more familiar terrain. But the route he and I must travel in order to arrive at fully analyzed prescriptions for U.S. policy is a good deal more complicated and problematical than he seems to appreciate.

In order to find the way, you must begin by knowing where you are. From what vantage point should we view U.S. interests? Professor van den Haag's formulation quoted above is ambiguous because in the realm of foreign policy, words like *costs, gain,* and *benefits* mean different things to different people. They are no more useful as guidelines to practical policy than airy references to "the national interest." We know that van den Haag does not see illegal behavior as a cost generator. Both from his other writings and from his tone here I conclude that he is not inclined to factor moral consequences into his calculus of national interest. Rather, as far as one can tell, he is concerned primarily with the impact of events on the wealth and power of the United States. Thus, he seems to place himself squarely within the classical tradition of *real politik.* Perhaps he would accept the slightly broader formulation proposed by that particularly celebrated defender of the Realist tradition, George Kennan: Statesmen must act on the assumption "that the state should be sovereign, that the integrity of its political life should be assured, that its people should enjoy the blessings of military security, material prosperity and a reasonable opportunity for . . . the pursuit of happiness."

With respect to the components of the policy equation, Professor van den Haag and I differ, it would appear, on two grounds. I believe that the perceived immorality and/or illegality of policy has strategic consequences. He does not. I believe that a democratic government has an obligation to pursue ends determined by the electorate and that, in the case of the United States, those ends include concern for the humanitarian impact of our policies. He does not.

I have already elaborated in general terms the potentially adverse consequences of indisputably illegal policies. Let us turn now to the particular case of Nicaragua. By organizing and underwriting an attempt to alter fundamentally, practically speaking to overthrow, that country's government, the United States violates two fundamental and closely related norms of contemporary international relations. One is the norm of respect for the sovereignty of states within their respective territories. The other is the norm of nonuse of force except for purposes of individual or collective self-defense. Since the prohibition of military aid to rebels is a universally recognized corollary of these norms, we violate it as well.

Both liberal and conservative administrations in Washington have repeatedly affirmed the universality of these norms, and they have frequently indicted other countries, particularly the Soviet Union, for violating them. To be sure, we have occasionally honored them in the breach, but in general we have complied because in general they serve the short, medium, and long-term interests of the United States.

As the leading actor in the international commercial world, the United States has an interest in stability that far exceeds that of the Soviet Union. Civil wars imperil both our diverse commercial interests and the army of American nationals abroad at all times in pursuit of personal as well as financial ends. Changes in technology have increased the power of the modern state to the point where rebellion is extraordinarily difficult without external assistance. A rule prohibiting such assistance is decidedly to our advantage to the extent that it exerts any significant influence on the behavior of other states.

Professor van den Haag will doubtless respond by noting that the Soviets and their allies have not infrequently violated it. To be sure, our own hands are not entirely clean. But surely the issue is whether the rule works at all, not whether it works all the time. No important rule does in any society.

I am confident that it has inhibited U.S. activity. I believe it has had some influence on the Soviets and their clients, if for no other reason than its sanctified status in the third world, where both superpowers compete for influence. One of the rule's demonstrable achievements has been complicating Cuba's efforts to reintegrate itself into the community of Latin American states. Whenever Cuba is seen to be back in the revolution-exporting business, its respectability among Latin states diminishes.

Whatever the rule's impact on Soviet behavior in the early postcolonial period when practically the entire third world was linked to the West, future efficacy seems likely given the increased number of fragile governments (for example, in South Yemen, Angola, Ethiopia, and a number of smaller African states) that profess a Marxist or at least leftist orientation. In other words, there is now more symmetry of interest between the superpowers. However, ours remains considerably greater.

Inhibiting other states, however marginally, from contributing to global instability by aiding rebels is one reason for reinforcing rather than undermining its prohibition. The ubiquity of our citizens and business gives us a strong motive for reinforcing the whole cluster of antiforce norms. A second motive is our interest—part strategic, part commercial, part moral—in encouraging ultimate relaxation of the Soviet grip on Eastern Europe and Afghanistan through their transformation from satrapies into Finlands. As long as we assert the right to use force for the maintenance of ideologically congenial regimes in the Western Hemisphere, the Soviets are very unlikely even to bother calculating the costs of imperial control in areas contiguous to them. Regarding us as the Hertz and themselves as the Avis of international relations, the Soviets tend to mime our behavior. Were that not so, various of their more costly entanglements in the third world would seem little short of deranged.

The mobility of our population and the global reach of our commercial interests provide reasons for lawful behavior vis-à-vis Nicaragua independent of our interest in influencing the actions of other states. Private persons—"terrorists," as we call them—increasingly threaten the physical security of American citizens, as well as the security of their property and business transactions. Our people, while not by any means the only target among the populations of the various Western states, seem to predominate in this unhappy respect. The Soviet Union and certain of its allies provide assistance to some terrorist groups, but there is little if any evidence that targets are selected in Moscow even in the case of groups that rely on Soviet rather than Iranian, Syrian, Libyan, or other public patronage. Inseminated by one or another modern tragedy, both real and imagined, terrorist groups have lives and targets peculiarly their own.

By seeming to exercise decisive influence over the destinies of other peoples—an inevitable consequence of our wealth and power and global presence—we would tend in any event to attract the animus of the aggrieved. My concern is that the exercise of our power in a manifestly illegal way against a small state like Nicaragua, whose government, through its association with the overthrow of Somoza's dictatorship, retains some residue of goodwill particularly among young, third world intellectuals, reinforces that tendency of the disaffected to see us as transnational ogres. I raise this possibility, and it is no more than that, with diffidence, fully appreciating that it is an intuitive hypothesis, supportable at best by anecdote. As an argument, it must, therefore, carry little weight. However, since the virtue of dialectic is a capacity to smoke out a wider range of considerations than a monologue is likely to expose, I add its sylphlike presence to the discussion.

Only a handful of disaffected third world youth succumb to the virus of terrorism. The vast majority, whatever their sense of grievance, will get on with the business of carving lives out of the materials at hand, however unpromising. Among the educated, a not trivial proportion will enter politics or the public service and become part of the next generation's governing elite. Surely it cannot be in the long-term interests of the United States to plant in the minds of such people an enduring image of our country as a kind of international rogue elephant. At least where we can do so with little if any cost, we should rather allow the Soviet Union to obtain exclusive rights to that role.

A considerably less problematic consequence of pursuing the destruction of the Sandinista government through the medium of the Contras is further strain on the already loosened ties of the NATO Alliance. While the imperious policies of the comandantes have sharply eroded the body of enthusiastic supporters they once enjoyed in Western Europe, the end and instrument of our policy continue to command hostility among a large proportion of European socialists, social democrats, and liberals. They do not even enjoy uniform or very enthusiastic support among conservatives. American unilateralists, because they regard Western European governments as a burden unduly restricting the global application of American power, may see added virtue in any policy that further unravels Alliance ties. Since, aside from maintaining hegemony over Eastern Europe, the Kremlin has evinced no foreign policy interest greater than separating Western Europe from the United States, Comrade Gorbachev will celebrate this notional virtue with at least equal enthusiasm.

European opponents of American policy may not express their opposition in legal idiom. Many may not even be conscious of the legal issues as such. Their animus is more likely to derive from a diffuse perception that we are behaving improperly, that we are bullying and displaying a swaggering disdain for world opinion. But at the heart of these imprecise perceptions, animating them, there is the paradigm of order erected out of the ruins left by World War II and embodied in the U.N. Charter and other treaties. That order has been good for Western Europe, as it has been good for us. Within its framework we have managed unparalleled prosperity, social harmony, and, at least within the confines of the Atlantic community, peace. Naturally, many Europeans will be hostile to precedents challenging the central features of that order, above all, restraints on recourse to force.

Professor van den Haag belittles those restraints. There have, he avers, been 100 wars since World War II. I do not know how he computed this nice, round, catchy figure. I do know that most of the conflicts have been domestic, and virtually all have been localized in the third world. The contrast with the preceding 100 years, indeed the preceding 400 years, cannot easily be overdrawn.

As I have noted before, particularly in a society where law arises from consensus, the general content of legal norms will tend to coincide with widely shared moral values. But in particular instances divergence can occur, in part because the architects of legal norms, determined to facilitate enforcement, may have chosen not to carve out exceptions for anomalous cases. Where it contributes to moral ends, illegal behavior reduces its strategic costs.

For instance, a cost I have not yet mentioned is fracturing the rough consensus required in a relatively democratic society for underwriting costly foreign ventures. The professor recognizes the problem. One reason he rejects the invasion option is his conviction that domestic opinion will not support the long-term occupation of Nicaragua.

Among the peoples of the West, Americans have a peculiarly intense need to find moral elevation in their country's diplomacy. Anything less challenges a central tenet of the American ideology. Hence, the Reagan administration's relentless effort to portray the Sandinistas as butchers with a totalitarian vocation and the Contras as humanitarians with a democratic one.

I will be more charitable to Professor van den Haag than he has been to me; I will assume that he is too sophisticated to accept the administration's comic-book version of Nicaraguan realities. We do not have to speculate about the character of the men who command Contra troops. Some previously served in Somoza's National Guard, whose grotesque delinquencies are recorded in the first report on Nicaragua of the International-American Commission of Human Rights. Christopher Dickey—probably the most acute, knowledgeable, and undogmatic of American journalists who have covered Central America during the past decade—having studied them at first hand, describes the officers as men addicted to violence, practicing indiscriminate brutality. They have made war in a manner dictated by their character, a war marked by the torture and murder of civilians.

Intense United States pressure has forced the various fighting groups to declare their ultimate subordination to a civilian junta that includes leaders in the earlier struggle against Somoza. But given the stunning difference in character and values between the Contra commanders, on the one hand, and civilians like Alfonso Robelo and Arturo Cruz, on the other, theirs is a misalliance that victory would surely dissolve. The democratic reformers among the Contras would again find themselves odd men out, not only because United States influence over the Contra officers would diminish if the Sandinistas were routed, not only because interest among the generality of Americans would diminish in that event, but also because the many right-wing civilians who figure prominently in the Contra movement would work with their ideological counterparts in Washington to offset reformist appeals for continued support.

While I am prepared to believe (until he demonstrates the contrary) that van den Haag harbors no illusions about the Contras, he seems determined to indict me for naïveté about the Sandinistas. After rereading my opening argument with scrupulous care, I am unable to find a shred of language suggestive of the belief that the Sandinistas are poised coyly on the threshold of democracy waiting to be coaxed across. No reasonable person examining my actual words is likely to be any more successful in confirming the professor's silly claim.

I refer repeatedly to the government's authoritarian character, and I know it at first hand. Twice in the years following Somoza's fall I visited the country as a member of the Human Rights Commission of the OAS. A mere 18 months into the Sandinista era sharp deviations from the democratic model were already apparent. They are recorded in the commission's second report on Nicaragua (the first dealt with Somoza), which I helped to author.

The situation of human rights has deteriorated seriously since my last visit in 1983. I and others opposed military pressure in part because we believed, for reasons I developed in my opening argument, that such deterioration was a likely consequence. Without coming to grips with my analysis, Professor van den Haag simply declares that growing repression within Nicaragua stems exclusively from the comandantes' Leninist values.

Provisionally excluding clairvoyance as his means, I fail to see the basis for his implicit claim of privileged access to the Sandinistas' minds. Although I have had long and brutally frank conversations with a number of the comandantes and other important figures in the regime, I feel no comparable confidence in my own grasp of their purposes. Events since Somoza's flight are incompatible with the view that the Sandinistas are democrats *manqué*. On the other hand, to date neither their words nor their deeds compel belief that their ends are totalitarian. For they are at least equally compatible with the view that the Sandinistas are inspired more than anything else by the Mexican model of a political system tolerant of pluralism *to the degree it does not threaten one-party rule*.

Leaders do not, however, have to be fired by a totalitarian vocation in order to end up totalitarian. The heirs of the Mexican revolution fashioned their political order in a less difficult political environment using more pliable materials. To achieve a more ambitious set of social reforms, the Sandinistas must struggle against a more developed and self-conscious indigenous entrepreneurial class and a more powerful church. Their protestations of desire for peaceful coexistence with a lively private sector are not incredible. Few Latin American leftists are impressed by the workings of state capitalism in Cuba and the Soviet Union. They too can read the statistics denominating economic stagnation. But as I have noted on several occasions, a dynamic private sector will always demand, if not a formal share of political power, then at least substantial influence over the great range of social and economic decisions that influence profitability and the distribution of wealth. And the greater the governing elite's sympathy for egalitarian outcomes, the more it will have to do to reassure the owners and managers of private capital.

The Sandinista experience confirms the hypothesis that a politically castrated entrepreneurial class will disinvest. Through acts of desperation more than will, the comandantes could end up with another shabby version of the statist economy.

In short, I recognize that Sandinismo has internal dilemmas that could lead to attempts at totalitarian solutions irrespective of the present plans of the comandantes and irrespective of United States pressure. Is Professor van den Haag conversely prepared to recognize that the Sandinistas are not necessarily following a preconceived plan for extinguishing every source of political, economic, social, and cultural diversity? I think not.

One no doubt finds it easier to prescribe and defend policies in a landscape methodically stripped of ambiguity. But since the prescription will therefore have only an accidental relationship to reality, its ties to national interest will be equally accidental.

What is unambiguous about Nicaragua is its inherent geopolitical unimportance. It is too poor, too small, too much under the shadow of overwhelming American power to matter in the balance of East–West power were it not for Washington's determination to pump it full of significance. Despite this administration's manic efforts in that direction, Nicaragua still looks to most people in the West like a little backward country in a poor and neglected part of the globe.

The Soviet Union shows no signs of rising to our invitation to a confrontation in our own backyard. It invests just enough political and economic resources to keep the tar baby standing, confident that, as a consequence of our frustration and paranoia and ideology, it can leverage a far larger investment out of Washington.

Instead of being, as van den Haag asserts, a cheap way of bleeding Moscow, aid to the Contras imposes disproportionate costs on us. That is why I continue to find the weight of our strategic interests as well as moral concerns tilting against this form of involvement in Nicaragua's fate.

As an alternative I have proposed economic and political measures coordinated with our allies in Europe and the principal Latin American states. These measures are no less sticks than carrots. And they would be backed by threats of direct action in the unlikely event Nicaragua launched an armed attack against its neighbors or Soviet military units set up shop in the country. Nothing in the history of the United States' relationship with the Caribbean Basin makes those threats anything but credible. All this Professor van den Haag dismisses as ''appeasement,'' although without any effort to tell us why.

If anything other than blind hatred of revolutionary regimes lies behind his *ipse dixit*s, it must be the following assumptions: first, that nothing short of Stalinist tyranny at home coupled with puppetlike subordination to the Soviet Union will satisfy the co-mandantes, and second, that political systems organized by elites with a Marxist perspective evolve according to unchangeable and unchanging law. Both assumptions defy only reason and precedent.

In the six decades since the Germans bundled Lenin back to Russia in a boxcar, regimes claiming inspiration from Marx have adopted an impressive variety of strategies for governing society and powering the economy. The etiology of diversity has been self-interest in the light of local history and circumstance. Self-interest includes, of course, psychic gratification from moving society toward an idealized end. Guided by self-interest, the Poles have left much land in private hands, the Russians have left little; the Yugoslavs have encouraged migration, the East Germans have killed to prevent it; the Bulgarians slavishly follow the Soviet line in foreign policy, the Chinese almost reflexively oppose it.

Because society is a living organism ceaselessly changing with a force no political system can wholly contain, because the surrounding international system is constantly producing new threats and opportunities, and because the human animal, being reflective, can adjust its ideals in the light of its errors, self-interest has produced radical changes over time in the strategies of Marxist as well as other sorts of regimes. Changes have included dramatic diplomatic realignment, from alliance with the Soviet Union to bitter hostility, and domestic shifts from experiments with a rigidly egalitarian income structure to one more skewed than its counterpart in many capitalist countries.

Our present policies confirm the historically well grounded belief of Caribbean Basin leftists that the United States will foster the overthrow of any regime that deploys state power to effect highly egalitarian reform. If much of the American elite sees Jimmy Carter as an aberration, he is unlikely to have appeared otherwise to the Sandinistas. Their behavior has been predictable for persons conditioned by history and ideology to expect a U.S.-sponsored counter-revolution, and driven by the arguably adolescent need to assert their independence from the regional hegemony, to exact a kind of psychological reparation from the United States.

While they fight for sheer survival, they have no dilemmas. I am suggesting that we alter the incentive structure and thereby create dilemmas. By isolating them economically, we deny them the means for the social and economic transformation of Nicaragua. Manipulating the self-interest of foreign governments at minimum cost to your own is the essence of diplomacy. Only a naif would confuse it with appeasement.

# CHAPTER 4

# Professor Farer Cannot Be Persuaded: I Should Have Known

## ERNEST VAN DEN HAAG

---

### Response to: There Is Too an International Law and We Violated It in Nicaragua

Tom Farer in Chapter 3 contends that (1) there is an international law deserving the label "law"; (2) the United States violated that international law by supporting the "Contras" in Nicaragua; we should accept a nonappealable verdict by the International Court of Justice enjoining us to stop that support; (3) our support of the Contras in Nicaragua is politically wrong as well, and thus contrary to U.S. interests.

Let me deal with some of Professor Farer's *obiter scripta* before turning to his main argument. Incidentally, he accuses me of "parodying" him in my response to Chapter 1. But he does not give any instance in which I have done less than justice to any of his views. Analyzing them ordinarily is not parodying them, although, come to think of it, in this case it might be. At any rate, I think his arguments are bad enough as he states them. Intentionally parodying them would be painting the lily.

Professor Farer's generalizations about history are, shall we say, incautious. He believes that rulers strengthen the legitimacy of their regimes by establishing equality before the law. This may be the case since the French Revolution. But equality before the law, despite roots in the classical antiquity of Western society, was not needed to bolster the legitimacy of medieval regimes and did not prevail before the 18th century. I doubt that it prevailed in non-Western societies or contributed to the legitimacy of their regimes. One should avoid historical and geographical parochialism. We cannot attribute to equality before the law—however desirable—a historical role beyond that actually played.

I don't think Farer helps his case, such as it is, by paraphrasing Anatole France, ''the law, in its majestic equality, forbids rich and poor alike to sleep under bridges, and to steal bread.'' This ''mordant'' sarcasm only shows that the celebrated French writer did not understand the nature of law. Anatole France obviously objected to the generality of the law—nobody is allowed to sleep under bridges be he rich or poor—when clearly only the poor would want, or need, to sleep under bridges. Thus, despite the general formulation, the burden of the law falls on a specific group, here the poor. What Anatole France did not understand is that the burden of the law—of any general rule—always falls only on those who, for whatever reason, are tempted to break it. Laws restraining the untempted only, and not those tempted to break them, would be redundant. Thus, prohibitions are formulated in general terms, but the actual burden falls on those restrained by them, not on those not tempted. The general terms are needed because those tempted, who must be restrained, cannot usually be identified beforehand. Further, a law prohibiting stealing only by the poor would be inconsistent with our notions of equality before the law. The burden of the legal prohibition against the sale of alcoholic beverages is borne by (would-be) drinkers, not by teetotalers. And the prohibition of stealing hits would-be thieves (mostly poor people), not people who needn't be restrained from stealing because they already have, or can buy, everything they desire. A law may be unwise or unjust, but not because it restrains those tempted to break it. That is its purpose, Anatole France and his followers to the contrary notwithstanding.

As though misconceiving law were not enough, Professor Farer misconceives economics as well. He states that nobody would "weave blankets," instead of "growing food," unless relying on the "promise" that he can exchange the blankets for food. Professor Farer thinks this is analogous to the promises of international law, which allows nations to rely on one another. But there is no such promise to the blanket weavers. Professor Farer has confused a promise, which is a binding agreement, with an expectation, which can be disappointed without legal (or even moral) objection. The blanket weavers (indeed the producers of any economic good) often are disappointed in their expectations. They may not be able to sell their product so as to buy food. Expectations do not amount to promises, let alone laws. The blanket weavers have no enforceable claim against the food producer. They may go hungry with a lot of blankets in their inventories. So with "international law." It too does not create enforceable claims. Therefore it is not law.

We speak of a criminal law prohibiting anyone from doing something (e.g., stealing), or of public law ordering government officials to levy a tax or spend public money on something or other, or of tort law bindingly assigning liabilities, or of contract law determining how agreements become binding on the parties. All these types of law are interpreted by courts and are enforced, by their orders, through the police. But international law? It is followed only when the parties volunteer to follow it. Every nation interprets it as it wishes—unless it *volunteers* to submit to an interpretation by some agreed-upon body. Nations volunteer only when it is in their interest to do so, or, at least, unlikely to injure their interests in important ways. Surely customs create expectations. But only when backed by the courts do these expectations become enforceable domestically. Internationally, they are not enforceable at all, unless all parties, including the party accused of acting contrary to custom or international law, volunteer to submit the dispute to some author-ity and volunteer to abide by its judgment. No such volunteering is needed to enforce a domestic law. The accused party cannot decline to appear, or to accept the jurisdiction or the judgment of the court, which is enforced by the police. International law is not even en-forceable in principle (let alone in practice) and to call it law is simply to confuse law with the things Professor Farer confuses law with, mainly customary expectations, or even agreed-to expecta-tions, or, finally, mutual promises that are not enforceable and therefore are binding only so long as the parties want to be bound.

This is not a mere dispute about words. Rather, my view ex-plains why "international law" cannot now settle any major con-flict among nations: It does not provide the means. Nor will international law ever be able to do so as long as nations remain sovereign. Professor Farer's use of the word *law* fosters the illusion that international law could solve major conflicts or substitute legal disputes for foreign policies. Worse, he advocates that we should submit to adverse judgment by international "courts," even though no one else does so if it is contrary to his interests. Could we really expect the Soviet Union to submit to international law? or North Korea? or East Germany? They never have in the past. Nor has Albania, Iraq, Iran, Israel, Argentina, or any self-respecting government.

To demonstrate that international law exists, Professor Farer writes: "Foreign policy bureaucracies cannot be satisfactorily ex-plained in any other way." One might as well say that God exists because ecclesiastical bureaucracies cannot be satisfactorily ex-plained in any other way. This is not a convincing way of demon-strating the existence of God, or of law. The existence of the respective bureaucracies only shows that some people *believe* that God, or international law, exists (wherefore they engage in pro-pitiatory rituals), not that they do.

Were it not for international law, Professor Farer proclaims, triumphantly quoting Robert Tucker, we should have invaded the

OPEC countries when they cartelized oil marketing and jacked up the price of oil. How superstitious can you get? Invasion would have been easy. But occupation would have been far more costly—in view of the guerrilla war and sabotage that oil installations can be subjected to—than the cost of the OPEC price increases. Sure, in the past occupation would have been cheap. But as a result of the rise of nationalism—not of international law—it is far too costly to be warranted now. That is why England preemptively left India and Ireland. England finds it costly now to continue occupying even that part of Ireland in which an overwhelming majority insist on remaining part of Great Britain.

Farer goes on to write that those "in favor of the abolition of military force except as an instrument of self-defense...codified their triumph in the U.N. Charter and the judgment of the Nuremberg Tribunal condemning wars of aggression." But the point is that despite the "triumph," neither the charter nor the Nuremberg trials prevent aggression. Indeed, without aggression "military force as an instrument of self-defense" would not be needed. We no longer even punish the defeated as was done at Nuremberg.

The "codification" Professor Farer triumphantly writes of confirms that international law is but a fantasy. It has neither prevented wars nor even led to judgments against aggressors, let alone to enforceable judgments. Nothing prevents Professor Farer and his colleagues from writing books about a nonexisting subject, or the bureaucracies from getting together and play-acting in the role of judges. But this scarcely helps people in Afghanistan, Iraq, Iran, Lebanon, Israel, or Cyprus. And it didn't help the Czechs, Hungarians, Cambodians, Tibetans, or Falklanders. How could it? The verdicts, if pronounced at all, are not enforced.

The United States refused to support the Anglo-French invasion of Egypt, as Farer points out. Later on, we did not use force against Khomeini, as Farer notes. In both cases we were wrong if we based our policy on international law, though we may have had more realistic reasons that I have to forego discussing. (However, it

seems clear to me that the Eisenhower–Dulles veto of the Anglo-
French-Israeli attempt to stop the Egyptian seizure of the Suez
Canal was foolishly contrary to our interests.)

Farer is probably right in noting that "actions [by the United
States] plainly prohibited by international treaty or custom, yet arguably cost-effective on other grounds, have failed to surface [I
guess he means to be considered] at high [U.S.] policy-making
levels." This may be one good reason for keeping lawyers away
from the U.S. Department of State.

When Hitler and Stalin attacked, the irrelevance of international law became clear. After they had been defeated the Nazis,
but not the Communists, were tried. The reason for the omission is
simply that the Communists were among the victors. Thus, the Soviets sat in judgment over the Nazis together with the Western allies, although the Soviets had conspired with the Nazis to attack
Poland, thereby starting World War II. No one even thought of
indicting the Soviets for their attack on Finland, let alone their occupation of Polish territory, or their later conquest and annexation
of the Baltic nations.

Nazi Germany indeed violated both German law and international custom—for which the Nazis certainly should be held to account. But no other government ever was held to account in modern
times. At Nuremberg the Nazis also were found guilty of waging
"aggressive war" and of "crimes against humanity." They were
guilty indeed. The trial was fair, except for one thing. There has not
been, and there is not now, operational law prohibiting aggressive
war or crimes against humanity—as the Vietamese, Cambodians,
Soviets, or Afghans can certainly testify. To be sure, all nations
have sworn off aggression or crimes against humanity. Unfortunately, nothing makes these agreements binding. They are not
enforceable. Each nation interprets them as convenient to it. An
odd kind of law, better called lawlessness.

Farer maintains that international law helps us predict how nations behave, *ergo* international law is "law." But suppose predic-

tions of behavior were based, as they sometimes are, on such things as economics, history, national character, or national interest—all of which are at least as reliable as predictive factors as what Farer chooses to call "international law." If it is predictive value that makes law, as Farer maintains, should national interest or economic interest be defined as law? Justice Holmes (whom Farer quotes), referring to domestic law, did not assert that law helps us to predict how people behave, which would be analogous to Farer's assertion about nations. Holmes, whom Farer here misinterprets, said only that law helps us to predict how courts of law will behave (which is true, unless courts are "activist," i.e., disregard the law). How courts behave is quite irrelevant to our discussion.

Farer points out, quite correctly, that I do not think international law is law because it is not authoritatively and bindingly interpreted or enforceable even in principle. But I do not deny that customs and treaties are voluntarily followed when convenient, just as, when one makes a date, one usually keeps it. But dates are not binding and do not have force of law; they can be unilaterally abrogated. They do not have the characteristics usually associated with law. Calling habitual behavior, or behavior the parties agree to, law, simply because it is likely to be adhered to and leads to the expectation of adherence is, shall we say, confusing. A voluntary agreement, or custom, is just that, and not law, even if it shares with law the characteristic of causing expectations. Unlike law, such an agreement or custom is not binding, adjudicable, or enforceable; at least international law is not.

On Nicaragua I differ with Farer on (1) what our interests are, (2) whether or not it is in our interest to pursue our interests by helping the Contras, (3) whether or not following "international law" is an important interest of ours, and (4) whether international law is at all relevant to the matter. I have already discussed (3) and (4).

As to (1): We must prevent another Soviet outpost, such as Cuba, in our hemisphere. Soviet penetration of Nicaragua is contrary to the pursuit of all our interests in Central and South America. It fosters anti-U.S., pro-Soviet insurrections, and the establishment of Soviet outposts in Latin America. This is what happened with Cuba, where we intervened too late, and in the wrong manner, having been lulled to sleep by *The New York Times* and by Professor Farer's colleagues. Cuba has since become a Soviet military outpost, sending its troops around the globe to increase Soviet power, which endangers ours. We are reduced to helping anti-Soviet elements in Africa and the Caribbean with some arms against Cuban-supported regimes. The Cubans support these pro-Soviet regimes with troops.

Helping the Contras is the most effective way of preventing Soviet consolidation in Nicaragua. Nicaragua has built up a disproportionate military force (as has Cuba), which threatens its neighbors. It is ridiculous to pretend that that force is meant to defend against an American invasion, against which it would be quite powerless. Whether or not the Contras succeed in overthrowing the Sandinista regime, they prevent its consolidation and any external use of its military power. The only reason we do not have Contras elsewhere is lack of opportunity—not international law. But we do finally support something like the Contras in Angola, Mozambique, and Cambodia—and we should do more. It seems too late to fight in Cuba or, for that matter, the Soviet Union.

Of course, the Soviets use what opportunities they can find. They will help their "Contras" in El Salvador or Colombia; they helped Vietnam and North Korea; they follow what Professor Farer quaintly calls *realpolitik* (as though there were an alternative to reality). We don't and often we pay the price of not having a real policy defending our real interest, instead of being deluded by the fantasies of "international law" that Professor Farer is trying to foist on us.

Surely, being realistic does not exclude concern for human rights, i.e., the avoidance of mistreatment of individuals and groups. In Nicaragua, in Cuba, and in the Soviet Union itself, violations of human rights are sponsored by Soviet power, exercised directly or through surrogates. Which is another reason to support the Contras. No doubt, the Contras themselves engage in acts of cruelty that are characteristic of civil wars. But just as Somoza's regime was mild compared to the Sandinista regime, just as the czar was a humanitarian compared to Lenin and Stalin, just as Battista was a benevolent gentleman compared to Castro, so the Sandinistas will be far worse than the Contras are likely to be.

I shall forever treasure Professor Farer's remark that "the Soviets tend to mime our behavior," which, according to Farer, explains "their more costly entanglements in the third world"— as though they need us to make mistakes. I wish they did "mime" our behavior. It would solve many problems and be a great advance for human rights in the world. Unfortunately, the mistakes, standards, and aims of the Soviet government are in most respects quite different from ours. Wherefore we have oppression of individuals and lack of political freedom in the Soviet Union. Soviet foreign policy reflects the aim of the regime to expand indefinitely and to consolidate its power, whereas our foreign policy is basically defensive — aimed at protecting ourselves and our allies from invasion or subversion by the Soviet government. It should be clear that the foreign policy of neither power has much to do with "international law."

To return to Nicaragua: Professor Farer sings the old song. The Sandinistas may go either way. They are not democrats, but so far they have not been shown, beyond a reasonable doubt, to be totalitarians. Perhaps they will be satisfied with a political monopoly à la Mexico, without descending into Soviet totalitarianism. This is the sort of thing we were told about Cuba. We were also told that if we were nicer to Castro he would become less pro-Soviet. Only now, when it is much too late, has he been willing to admit that he was a Communist all along, never had any inclinations except pro-Soviet ones, and simply found it profitable to deceive those who wanted to be deceived. Why tolerate a repetition of the same scenario? Can't we ever learn?

I do not know to what extent the Sandinistas have a "preconceived plan" in their minds. Some may be ambivalent, others not. But the facts—confiscation of the property of opponents, imprisonment of opponents, harassment of the Roman Catholic Church and expulsion of its bishops, suppression of the freedom of the press—speak for themselves. As the Sandinistas lose more and more popular support as a result of their harebrained economic policies and of the military draft, they will have to resort to more and more totalitarian policies to keep their power. Surely not even Professor Farer envisages that they will allow themselves to be peacefully replaced, even in part, by a democratically elected non-Sandinista government. As they pursue totalitarian policies they will tolerate dissent less and less (note Cuba), and they will come to rely on the Soviet Union (see Cuba) more and more. They will have to pay the same price Cuba pays: help the Soviets as much as possible to bring communism to South and Central America and to the Caribbean. They will not have to send troops to Africa only because they cannot afford to, even with Soviet subsidies. But without the Contras, the Sandinistas will help pro-Communist guerrillas wherever they have an opportunity, and, whenever possible, they will try to create such guerrillas. Fortunately, the Contras absorb enough of the Sandinistas' resources to make it hard for them to help guerrillas elsewhere. Without the Contras the Sandinistas would be all over.

South and Central America is badly enough governed to create plenty of discontent on which guerrilla movements can thrive. But bad as the current authoritarian governments are in many Latin American countries, we have no reason to help the guerrillas institute worse ones. By failing to help the Contras in Nicaragua we would enable the Sandinistas to do so.

Professor Farer is right in saying that Nicaragua has no geopolitical importance *per se* except (as he does not say) if the Soviets were to install a naval base there, which so far they have not tried.

But Professor Farer does not seem to understand the political importance of Nicaragua as a guerrilla support base, which I have just described. There is no point in knocking down straw men, in pretending that I believe that Nicaragua is important otherwise and then refuting what I never asserted. Nicaragua is important politically—not because it threatens the United States militarily.

# III

CHAPTER 5

# Irreducible Differences?

## TOM J. FARER

---

The hope originally animating this dialogue begins to be realized. Professor van den Haag and I knew we disagreed about the policy of the Reagan administration. We believed that by dialectically defending our respective positions, we would end up exposing the values and assumptions from which our differences spring in this and other instances of contemporary American foreign policy. And we were indifferent as to whether the net result would be (1) a demonstration of more common ground than is immediately apparent between the right wing of Western politics, whose views Professor van den Haag accurately reflects, and the center left, represented I hope not too idiosyncratically (as distinguished from eccentrically) by me or, conversely, (2) a demonstration that we have little in common other than mutual good-natured tolerance.

One's position on any particular foreign policy issue is deeply influenced, I believe, by some sort of moral or aesthetic reflex, a finally unanalyzable preference for certain groups over others and for certain social and political arrangements. It resists definition in the same way as does a color. Yellow is, well, yellow. And it is as immune as a color preference to justification, and hence to argument. *De gustibus non est disputandum.* But this visceral inclination—often unconscious, rarely revealed—is connected to one's position in a given case by a lengthy skein of assumptions about cause and effect, about ways of perceiving facts and acquiring information, all in all about the way the world works.

Because they are invariably defended on reasoned grounds, in principle these assumptions are available for reasoned dispute. If we can demonstrate to their holder that they are mutually inconsistent or poor predictors of historical outcomes, in theory he or she should alter them. My hunch, however, is that the ultimate reflex of sympathy and revulsion influences the choice of assumptions, influences it so profoundly that few demonstrations will satisfy the holder. Among other things, then, this dialogue is a test of that hunch.

## The Legal Issue

It is above all with respect to the legal aspects of U.S. policy in Central America that Professor van den Haag and I have come closest to peeling back the epidermis and getting at the hard bone of our differences. To this point the issue has assumed a possibly surprising prominence in our discourse, surprising at least for the great number of people who, even if they do not quite share Professor van den Haag's views, nevertheless regard legal questions as a sideshow to the main event where we joust over moral and strategic questions.

Its prominence has at least three causes. One is the fact that although civil armed conflict with transnational implications has been a recurrent phenomenon of the past 40 years, this is the first case where one of the interested parties has invoked the jurisidiction of the International Court of Justice and actually secured a judgment from that august body. And although it cut and ran when the Court found it had jurisdiction and thus turned to the merits, the United States also has framed the case for its policies in legal terms, although not exclusively so. Given the peculiarly important place of litigation, judicial review, and the rule-of-law ideal in the ideology and actual operation of American democracy, Nicaragua's insistence on expressing its claims against the United States in legal form and its success in obtaining a judgment from just about as impartial an international tribunal as could probably be assembled on a broadly representative basis was bound to have a certain resonance within the United States, albeit much less than one might have hoped.

The prominence the issue has assumed in our discourse stems also from the relative sharpness and clarity of our differences, which in turn flow from Professor van den Haag's willingness to argue his case rather than simply to assert it. In this respect he has dealt very differently with moral, strategic, and tactical questions. As I will shortly attempt to demonstrate, when confronting those questions he has thus far failed to respond to the particularities of my arguments, preferring, it would appear, to dismiss summarily arguments that I either have not made at all or have made with various qualifications and shadings he chooses to ignore.

A third reason for prominence is, as I have already noted, the linkage between legal and all other issues, with the former encapsulating widely shared and carefully calculated perceptions of common national interests. In talking about the law, therefore, one is necessarily talking as well about every other kind of value, including, of course, those of a strategic and moral character.

On Professor van den Haag's side, there must be a great deal more to say about the legal issues we have raised; I assume there must be because, while he has argued his own case at some length, he has not really had a great deal to say about mine. His second round of argument largely restates the position he assumed in round one, a position I summarized as the belief "that law exists only where obligations . . . are interpreted and enforced by an authority independent of and both formally and practically superior to the obligated party.'' In other words, Professor van den Haag has postulated an institutional paradigm and then declared that any social system that does not conform to that paradigm has no law.

I, by contrast, have suggested that no useful end is served by an abusive discourse about abstract models. Whatever name one chooses to apply to the dense network of custom and formal agreement whose existence Professor van den Haag does not deny, the question for practical people concerned with shaping foreign policy is whether compliance with the norms embodied in those customs and agreements tends to advance the national interest. I have tried to show both in general and in the particular case of Nicaragua how compliance serves American interests. And I have explained in detail how the policy of the Reagan administration violates well-established norms. Since my colleague has not chosen to contest either my statement of the applicable law (out of conviction and for convenience I will dare to continue using that word) or my analysis of United States behavior in light of that law, I take it that neither point is in dispute. One must therefore conclude that he continues to support Reagan administration policy on the assumption that the violation of extant norms is cost-free or that whatever the costs, they are outweighed by the strategic and moral advantages to be gained in this instance from noncompliance.

I presume the former, as well as the latter, proposition expresses Professor van den Haag's views. Precisely why he rejects my several hypotheses about the cost of violating applicable norms in this case is not altogether clear. Reading through his second round of responses one finds oneself not so much identifying his arguments as reconstructing them, very much in the way an archeologist imagines the character of an object by extrapolating from available shards. I could not tell, for example, whether he accepted my contention (based on personal experience and study of the foreign policy process, particularly in the United States) that the senior officials who, through their action and advice, actually implement foreign policy are influenced by the tolerances and constraints of what they take to be international law. I could not tell because, rather than addressing this empirically verifiable proposition, he dismisses its relevance.

Dismissal might reflect a failure of understanding. Professor van den Haag quotes me as writing, in order to demonstrate the existence of international law, that "foreign policy bureaucracies cannot be satisfactorily explained in any other way." What I had actually written was that "the *structure and functioning* of foreign policy bureaucracies cannot be satisfactorily explained in any other way" (new emphasis). I was arguing, of course, that the time officials spent studying the legal implications of their decisions and advice evidenced *belief* that law existed and that it was sufficiently important to be taken into account. That much Professor van den Haag seems to grasp inasmuch as he finds it useful to declare, "The existence of the respective bureaucracies only shows that some people *believe* that God, or international law, exists (wherefore they engage in propitiatory rituals), not that they do."

Naturally I agree that the existence of, to take his analogy, ecclesiastic bureaucracies does not demonstrate the existence of God. So what! God is external to human ways of being and knowing. But *belief* in Him of course does have material consequences in the secular world. Similarly, material consequences flow from the belief, on the part of persons who play a not negligible role in the formation of foreign policy, that certain customary and treaty-defined behavior is not merely predictable but is obligatory (because of an underlying and universal agreement to treat norms meeting certain criteria as commands), and that deviance has costs. Perhaps Professor van den Haag thinks that the world would be better off without such beliefs. For the reasons I developed in Part II, such beliefs are a corollary of an international system with more or less fixed participants just as they are an incident of life in an isolated village. But even if I am wrong in claiming that the emergence of such beliefs is inevitable in any stable society, even if it would be a better world had such beliefs never arisen, nevertheless, if, as I contend, they do exist, anyone wishing to function effectively in the practical world of foreign policy must take account of them.

The nub of Professor van den Haag's darting argument, I believe, is that the costs of deviance are slight. And they are slight, even negligible, because deviance is commonplace and, moreover, expected, particularly where compliance requires the sacrifice of important national interests. "No self-respecting government," he proclaims, will "submit to international law," meaning, I take it, that they shouldn't and they won't and they don't.

Professor van den Haag supports this claim in two ways: by invoking notorious violations of the force-regulating norms I have sketched and by implicitly positing a sort of law of human nature according to which no rational leaders will ever sacrifice prospective gains for the national interest simply in order to satisfy the expectations of other sets of leaders. The trouble with this law, from Professor van den Haag's perspective, is its irrelevance to his argument. It is irrelevant because it does not bear on the question of whether political leaders might in fact promote national interests by complying with those expectations that have hardened into a collective sense of obligation. If, as I have argued, deviance does have costs, it follows that compliance, where it occurs, is premised not on the intrinsic good of satisfying the legitimate expectations of other states but rather on the comfortably crass grounds of fostering the interests of one's own.

I will not test the reader's patience by recapitulating my entire argument about the advantage of compliance and the costs of deviance. But since much of Professor van den Haag's response seems to slide by its main points, I will try one final summary in the hope of provoking either agreement or a dissent that meets me at all points.

Interstate relations, like the relations between people, are a mix of competition and cooperation, of conflicting and shared interests. *Law* is the term we give to the rules and principles that develop—in some cases all at once through explicit agreement, in others gradually as states applaud, tolerate, or condemn each other's behavior with respect to some issue until there emerges an implicit consensus about the limits of national discretion—to facilitate cooperation and to hold competition within limits that do not threaten widely shared interests. Wherever in the relations of states interests conflict so sharply as to thwart consensus about the limits of tolerable behavior, anarchy reigns, subject, however, to certain all-inclusive rules, such as that requiring the exhaustion of non-violent remedies before threatening extreme forms of coercion even in order to vindicate unambiguous legal rights.

States agree to abide by those rules that will, in the generality of cases, promote their respective interests. In exceptional cases, however, a rule will seem to obstruct some policy initiative calculated to optimize gains for a particular state. Appearance and reality may not in fact coincide. World history is littered with the ruins deposited by legions of erroneous calculations of national interest. Particularly when governments believe that the time for decision is limited, they may act on the basis of very inadequate information, or fail to think through all the consequences of a proposed initiative. And governments may be unduly influenced by factors whose long-term insignificance is not immediately apparent. *Since legal norms express unhurried calculations of national interest, it would seem that leaders could best serve that interest by placing the burden of persuasion on those urging noncompliance.*

Nevertheless, exceptional cases will arise where the potential gains from violating the terms of a treaty or the unambiguous limits of a well-grounded custom, even if other states respond with equivalent violations, create an irresistible temptation. (Similarly in the domestic context, a driver carrying a desperately ill spouse to the hospital may well not resist the temptation to run a red light. The temptation will no doubt be less if running red lights has become commonplace.) Of course, if acts of noncompliance multiply—and one act does encourage others—expectations of compliance will sink to the point where the violated norm is seen to have expired.

From the beginning of our dialogue I have, in effect, been asking Professor van den Haag whether he really believes that the United States or any other nation could more effectively promote the general welfare of its citizens in a world where states lacked the means consciously to increase the predictability of their interactions. For the celebration of just such a world is implied by the denial that a proposed policy's inconsistency with a rule satisfying the agreed-upon criteria for making and identifying a rule of law is not itself a substantial reason for rejecting the proposal. In such a world, treaties would have no place, since their existence would in no appreciable degree increase the likelihood of desired behavior. The arduous work of negotiating and ratifying them would be a waste of time. Because such a world would be far more dangerous and less productive than the one in which we actually live, governments will go on, despite Professor van den Haag's protestations, creating law and, in general, complying with it in part for no worse reason than the fact that it is law.

Like participants in domestic legal systems, states will construe treaty provisions and customary rules in the manner most favorable to themselves, but in doing so they will, if they are prudent, recognize, first, that whatever claims they make will be invoked by other states as justifications for similar behavior, and, second, that if they press interpretation beyond the limits other states deem reasonable in light of established principles of interpretation, they may be undermining an agreement or customary rule that is in general beneficial. And as in every system of law, calculations or miscalculations of self-interest will sometimes lead to outright delinquency.

Since, so far as we know, there never has been a legal system free of deviant behavior, I wonder why Professor van den Haag believes he has made a point when, somewhat indiscriminately, he invokes violations of international law. In light of the opportunities for tangible self-aggrandizement relatively powerful states experience daily, the cases enumerated by him, so elliptically that I am not always sure to which incident he is referring, seem trivial in number. Every day, as Professor Louis Henkin of Columbia University once pointed out, the United States chooses not to invade Canada despite that country's great lode of natural resources, military weakness, and independent foreign policy. Is law the explanation of our restraint? Not entirely. Not even primarily, I would suppose. But law tangibly expresses the complex of factors that have led even the powerful to see merit in inhibiting recourse to force. And in cases where the rules are absolutely clear, law reinforces decisions made on other grounds in other circumstances where the temptation may have been less. As I noted earlier, law helps keep certain options off the decision-making agenda.

Perhaps it is Professor van den Haag's intention to suggest that only some countries are influenced by law, countries like ourselves, who thus place themselves at a competitive disadvantage. "Could we really expect the Soviet Union to submit to international law?" he asks rhetorically. "They never have in the past," he claims, without offering a shred of proof to support so broad and peremptory a claim.

In the area of arms control, for example, Soviet behavior seems not much different from our own. We and they have interpreted agreements in ways each government has deemed beneficial to its presumed strategic interests. Each of us has pushed against the limits of language and negotiating history, and neither has always honored the spirit of agreements. In the case of the ABM treaty, the Soviets have built a radar whose compatibility with the treaty is very uncertain, while we now claim the right to test defensive weapons in space despite treaty language that on its face would seem to preclude it. Nevertheless, both of us have thus far abided by the main limitations of the various agreements.

If we did not believe that formally ratified agreements were more likely than informal understandings with the Soviet Union to secure compliance, why would we bother investing in such agreements vast amounts of senior decision-making time and domestic political capital? Conversely, if the Soviets took the view of Professor van den Haag that compliance is purely voluntary and that everyone expects them to withdraw whenever it appears that by doing so they can grab some strategic advantage, why wouldn't they then agree to provisions strongly desired by the United States just in order to secure restraints on U.S. behavior, planning all the while to evade burdensome restraints through cheating or sudden withdrawal or a bad-faith plea of changed circumstances or fanciful interpretation? The fact is that despite a great deal of mutual suspicion, each believes that formal legality minimizes the risk of arbitrary withdrawal or evasion.

Their respective acceptance of the contemporary world's basic institutional structure leads both superpowers to acquiesce in a whole range of legal inhibitions. Although the Soviets depend far more than we on the sea for protein, they respect the 200-mile national fishing zones that have evolved since World War II. Rather than escorting their fishing fleets with warships, they act like states unendowed with powerful fleets: They purchase licenses.

The Soviet Union, like many other states, does not accept the compulsory jurisdiction of the World Court. But it has accepted arbitration of commercial disputes involving state agencies.

Unfortunately for Professor van den Haag, the real world does not submit to his neat dichotomies. Unfortunately for the world, states of all sorts will sometimes act as he would have them always act; they rip through the fabric of law in search of at best short-run, at worst illusory gains. Thus the United States has organized the overthrow of one democratically elected government in Guatemala (1954) and colluded in the overthrow of another in Chile (1970–?), as well as organizing the invasion of Cuba (1961) and actually invading the Dominican Republic (1965), relying in part on an invitation about as legally relevant as the ones invoked by the Soviet Union when it invaded Afghanistan and, earlier, Hungary and Czechoslovakia. We nevertheless continue to think of ourselves as an essentially law-abiding state because, in the generality of our relations with other states, we do adhere to the law. I expect that the Soviets feel very much the same, although, given their history and ideology, their impulse to comply may well be more purely instrumental in character than ours.

Nothing I have said at any point amounts to the claim that "international law can settle major conflicts" or "substitute legal disputes for foreign policies." Obviously it cannot *substitute* for foreign policy, any more than law within nations replaces individual strategies for the pursuit of success in business, love, or any other realm of human activity. While excluding certain means and ends, law leaves both states and individuals with a wide range of discretion in the choice of tactics, strategies, and goals. It canalizes ambition and passion and through its limits helps to prevent the sort of destructive competition that impoverishes all of the players; it also facilitates cooperation by lending special force to certain forms of agreement. Being made by players weaned on competition, the law's vocation is not to eliminate competition but rather to regulate it for the mutual benefit of its creators.

And obviously it cannot settle conflicts. But it can provide a means for avoiding conflicts in that it sketches the limits of what states may do without provoking retaliation. In addition, it provides an effective way for political leaders to resist intemperate constituents urging vindication of perceived rights or interests without reference to cost. Chile and Argentina, for example, avoided war over the Beagle Channel islands by submitting their dispute to the Pope not for an arbitrary or merely equitable decision but for one guided by the rules and principles of international law.

Disputes over strategically and materially trivial issues have sparked many a conflict at a cost to all participants out of all proportion to any rational calculus of the national interest. Law helps us to recognize the difference between a mere glancing collision of legitimate interests and a threat to the whole system of international order. And it offers a means of saving face for states that, having stepped into quagmires without due regard for consequences, have come at last to their senses.

I rest my case, which is, after all, no more than the proposition that in organizing, arming, training, and otherwise supporting the so-called Contras, the United States is violating international law and that that is a substantial reason for terminating support. Indeed, it is sufficient, unless someone persuasively demonstrates that termination would mean sacrificing very important strategic and/or moral interests of the United States. I do not believe that Professor van den Haag has made or can make that requisite demonstration.

## The Strategic Issue

Here I think Professor van den Haag and I have thus far failed to clarify *in depth* the causes of our division. Why? Perhaps because, to judge from his comments so far, he finds the strategic case for aid to the Contras so clear as to dispense with the need for extended argument. In his mind, it comes simply to this: The Sandinista government, through an act of ideologically guided choice, has made itself into an extension of Soviet power. The United States cannot alter that choice. Any extension of Soviet power threatens United States interests. Ergo, we must alter the regime or, if that cannot be accomplished at reasonable cost, weaken and distract it by facilitating the Contra insurgency. Moreover, since regimes of the Left are invariably more destructive of human rights than right-wing authoritarian governments, in the process of protecting United States security interests by preventing the consolidation of a Soviet clone, we incidentally contribute to human rights in Nicaragua.

The argument's economy is almost elegant. It expresses the common wisdom that the friend of my enemy is my enemy. But it takes no account of costs either to the United States or to the Soviet Union; its presumption concerning the disutility of measures other than force rests in large part on the further presumption, adopted in the face of disconfirming precedent, that ideology is a precise and unalterable determinant of policy; and, insofar as human rights are concerned, it rests on no persuasive factual grounds at all. Its simplicity, therefore, seems less like the fruit of inspiration than the failure of intellect.

Both my initial probe of the issues engaged by our efforts to destroy the Nicaraguan government and my response to Professor van den Haag's opening salvo developed at considerable length the various sorts of costs that administration policy incurs and the possible virtues of alternative means for the pursuit of American ends, while at the same time examining the ends we might wisely pursue. My colleague has not so much discussed my views as pelted them with a few carefully culled chunks of history.

History in its Delphic majesty rarely speaks clearly other than when reminding us of the stunning diversity of human events and their corresponding reluctance to repeat themselves. One thing it certainly does not do is support the several claims essential to Professor van den Haag's position: the claim that leftist regimes evolve relentlessly toward totalitarian control of society; the claim that leftist revolutionaries inevitably support the Soviet Union; the claim that once regimes fall or step into the Soviet orbit, they cannot be induced to withdraw; the claim that revolution in one third world country places virtually all nonrevolutionary governments in the region seriously at risk.

Like the Bourbons in some respects, Professor van den Haag differs in the selectivity of his recall. China under Deng Xiaoping, Yugoslavia during and after Tito, Hungary in 1956, Czechoslovakia in 1968—all exemplify not merely authoritarian leftist, but full-fledged Communist Party-run regimes evolving *toward* greater pluralism. In both the Czechoslovakian and Hungarian cases, the internal dynamics of regime and society were pushing the countries rapidly toward nothing less than open societies with competitive politics when the Soviets invaded to abort the process. As Communist elites have sometimes eased their grip on society, even in the face of domestic challenge to their style of governance, comparable challenges have not infrequently inspired conservative ones to tighten theirs: most conspicuously Germany and Italy before World War II, various Latin American capitalist–military alliances in the 1960s and early 1970s, and South Africa today, to name only some.

History no less clearly demonstrates that revolutionary regimes do not invariably end up as Soviet consorts. Like the Chinese and Albanians, they may be actively hostile or, like the Yugoslavs, Mozambicans, and Zimbabweans, they may opt for neutral space between East and West, either immediately after seizing power or only after the Soviet link begins to inhibit attainment of personal and national goals. In some instances, the West has done nothing to facilitate the loosening of ties, has failed even to recognize divorce until well after the event. In others, it has actively contributed. The prospect of economic aid and assistance in dealing with South Africa helped shift Mozambique further from Soviet influence (it had never been an intimate collaborator). By contrast, it was only after the United States had, in a fit of good sense, refused to underwrite the military necessities of the Ethiopian Stalinist, Mengistu Haile Mariam, that he appealed to the Soviet Union.

The historical record is equally unkind to the implied claim that if not all the third world, then at least much of Latin American is so much dry grass awaiting the revolutionary spark. It is hard to tell who was more surprised in the 1960s, we or the Cubans, to learn that rather than being dry grass, the hemisphere's social terrain was more akin to a swamp. Che Guevara discovered this error in the miserable, illusion-cracking days before it swallowed him. The Soviets never made it. Their disparagement of the whole revolution-exporting enterprise brought them into collision with Fidel Castro, who publicly castigated his presumed masters for an insufficiency of guts. Only gradually did disillusion and dependency bring Fidel into line with the Soviet view that, Latin American not being in a prerevolutionary condition, Communist parties

should participate in electoral coalitions and Communist governments should seek friendly state-to-state relations with their Latin
counterparts.

In my skepticism about Nicaragua's alleged role as the fuse of
revolutions all over the Caribbean Basin, if not all the way to Tierra
del Fuego, Professor van den Haag hears echoes of "the old song,"
presumably the one he thinks he heard liberals singing at the time of
the Cuban revolution. Actually, it was a covey of "liberals" who,
fearing the spread of revolution, dispatched guns and cash to Latin
America and set up counterrevolutionary schools for Latin scoundrels, all in the name of prophylaxis. The favorite song of the time
was "Revolution is a-comin', so you better watch out."

Just about the time it slipped off the Western Hemisphere hit
parade, liberals and rightists burst into song in Saigon. As Indochina goes, we were told, so goes Southeast Asia. Lyndon Johnson
had dominoes falling all the way to Honolulu. Well, Indochina fell,
and its southern neighbors—Thailand, Malaysia, Singapore, and
Indonesia—seem never to have been so stable and secure.

Even at the peak of their export-the–revolution rhetoric, when
Mao was verbally conscripting every third world cluster of starving
insurgents into his grand army of liberation, the Chinese insisted
that revolutions were not susceptible to export, that they had to be
made by local people responding to local conditions, if they were to
be made at all. What history does seem to confirm repeatedly is
that, despite all the misgovernment Professor van den Haag rightly
sees on every side, they are rarely made at all.

So if, as my colleague argues, the past is prologue, his principal justification for attributing strategic importance to a leftist government in Managua implodes. He would be better off arguing that,
however many times wolf was erroneously cried in the past, the old
lobo is at last at the door. To be frank, the obstacles to a persuasive
argument on this score are formidable. Most Latin countries have
more efficient military and civilian bureaucracies today than in the

early 1960s. In addition, the experience of repressive military governments and state terror have strengthened the commitment to democratic processes all along the political spectrum from socialist to moderate conservative and thereby strengthened barriers to the sort of political polarization that often prepares the ground for a serious revolutionary effort. Experience has also discouraged both millenarian goals and doctrinaire economic nostrums. A more moderate rhetoric, a more tolerant politics, a more pragmatic economics, more efficient governments, and, on top of all that, a still stronger commitment to the peaceful resolution of interstate disputes (exemplified by Argentina's acceptance of papal arbitration of its territorial dispute with Chile and the more recent cooperation agreement between Argentina and Brazil)—these are hardly the harbingers of a revolutionary tide.

Given Professor van den Haag's insistence, at the close of his last *tranche*, that "Nicaragua is important politically—not because it threatens the United States military...[but rather] as a guerrilla support base," I wonder why he quarrels with me about the size of the Nicaraguan army. It is not ridiculous, in any event, to suppose that size has some relation to the fear of an invasion either orchestrated or actually conducted by the United States. With proper training and materiel, Nicaragua would have a decent chance to repel a Contra invasion stiffened by CIA-organized mercenaries and "volunteers" recruited from friendly Central American governments before the invaders could convert themselves into a plausible alternative government by seizing and holding a substantial hunk of territory. Obviously the Nicaraguans could never hope to defeat an open invasion by U.S. forces, any more than Switzerland, despite its ability to mobilize quickly most of its able-bodied citizens, could have successfully resisted a German invasion during World War II. But the capacity to sustain resistance and inflict casualties can deter invasion, assuming the potential adversary is inclined to do its sums before acting.

As we disagree about the strategic dimensions of the Nicaraguan problem, so we disagree about the means available for containing it. Of course, I think those dimensions so slight that I would feel comfortable if the American nation would devote its limited attention, its feverish energy, its large but hardly limitless resources to other, more consequential, challenges. But if there is no way of altering the conventional conviction that "something must be done," then why not attempt the same trade with Nicaragua that the Soviet Union has made with Finland? If a country so determined, as Professor van den Haag would have it, to disseminate its system throughout the globe can live with ideological diversity on its frontiers, why must we writhe at the thought?

Even my colleague does not imagine Nicaragua's contributing troops in the Cuban style to Soviet-bloc adventures in the third world. Perhaps that is why he does not stir himself to explain why bloc expenditures in poorhouses of the globe like Ethiopia and Angola—which continue, in any event, to trade with the West—should be deemed a prudent application of limited resources. Nor, unlike certain hysterics who wander on the Right, does he project Nicaragua's conversion into a basing point for the Soviet armed forces. As I noted above, he rests his case on the prospect of a contagion of revolutions, though without explaining what Nicaragua would add to the resources Cuba has in the past been willing episodically to deploy for that end. And so I ask what I have asked throughout our exchange: Why not exchange U.S. tolerance for Nicaraguan neutrality?

Does he believe that ideology renders the Sandinistas compulsive propagators of revolution? What ideology do they have other than nationalism and a loose syncretic sort of Marxism? Ideology has not prevented them from relaxing their initial, and in many areas unpopular, land-reform emphasis on cooperatives in favor of land to its tillers, any more than Marxism has prevented the Chinese from unleashing market forces and tapping into the Western trading system rather than trying to bury it.

Professor van den Haag places virtually the entire weight of his argument on a single precedent, Cuba. Like many Americans, he is so obsessed by the capacity of this little island off the coast of

Florida to defy us that he unintentionally collaborates with Fidel Castro in recklessly inflating its importance on the scales of world power. Nicaragua, he appears to believe, is bound to follow the Cuban example and become a pliant tool of the Soviet Union; the latter will use the tool, as it uses Cuba, to propagate revolutions. Like Fidel, the Sandinistas will be driven by the imperatives of ideology and self-preservation.

As I noted above, revolutionary ideology has shown itself compatible with hostility to the Soviet Union and with nonalignment, as well as with strategic cooperation. In the Cuban case, survival rationality alone would have driven Fidel into close alliance with Soviet power. He intended a radical alteration of society and economy in his country. The result would be highly injurious to U.S. investors. Only four years before his triumph, the United States had organized the overthrow of President Jacobo Arbenz of Guatemala after he initiated reforms far more modest than the ones envisioned by Castro. Professor van den Haag implies that Castro required Soviet assistance to protect his government from indigenous opponents. But it is by no means clear that he could not have handled them without external aid. What he clearly did need a Soviet umbrella for was shelter from the United States. Since the United States never offered Cuba the Finlandization option, the Cuban experience is irrelevant to the question of whether we could successfully negotiate such an arrangement with the government of Nicaragua.

It is true that the Sandinistas began to display pro-Soviet sympathies as soon as they came to power (for example, by not voting to condemn the Soviet invasion of Afghanistan) and in the face of conciliatory moves by President Carter. Among other things, he drew on his declining stock of political capital to coax an economic aid package out of the hands of a reluctant Congress. There are, however, several equally plausible interpretations of Sandinista behavior. Having acquired power in a country that for some three-quarters of a century had been a *de facto* dependency of the United

States, a country whose national hero had been murdered by a United States client, they could have been venting a long-accumulating deposit of nationalist emotions, cocking a snook at the great northern hegemony for the sheer pleasure of the thing and in the expectation of sympathetic vibrations among the general population. Additionally, and not necessarily in the alternative, they may, like Castro before them, have assumed that within a short time, the United States would move against this, as it had moved against every other revolutionary project in the hemisphere.

While Castro had Guatemala freshly in mind, the Sandinistas had an additional augury of U.S. behavior—our collusion in the unsuccessful effort to organize a coup at the time of Salvador Allende's election to the Chilean presidency. Not only may they have seen Carter as an aberration certain to be swept aside by the natural movement of American policy; even during Carter's presidency, elements of the national security bureaucracy, acting on their own, may have opened contact with exiled Somocistas, contacts known to the Sandinistas. Since they were anticipating a U.S.-organized effort to unseat them unless they relinquished their domestic goals, prudence would dictate an effort to draw the Soviets into a protective relationship.

Fear of formidable domestic opposition might have impelled them to seek Eastern-block support *irrespective of their assumptions about U.S. policy.* But I doubt it, because Somoza's flight left them with a monopoly of force within Nicaragua, and their earned image as the vanguard of the anti-Somoza coalition left them with a reservoir of popular support. Moreover, they appeared to believe that planned initiatives in land reform, health, and education would consolidate their popularity with the great mass of workers and peasants, as well as urban middle-class youth. Like many predecessors in the adventure of radical reform, the Sandinistas seem to have underestimated both the strength of conservative instincts in the lower classes and the extent of the economic difficulties their policies would create.

Whatever their initial expectations, would the continuation of Soviet aid at present levels be required for their survival if the United States withdrew support from the Contras? I think Professor van den Haag believes the answer to that question is yes, an affirmative answer being a necessary condition of his claim that Nicaragua is bound to accept the status of a Soviet pawn. Judging from the absence of any supporting evidence, belief in this instance is just a leap of faith. While the consensus among those who regularly visit and systematically study the country is that Sandinista popularity is much diminished, even observers sympathetic to the Contras are impressed by their inability to inherit much of the support their opponents have relinquished. Hence, the emphasis among their American supporters on the need to develop an attractive political program and to obscure their connections to the Somoza era. The extent of Contra reliance on forced recruitment tends to substantiate this pessimistic assessment of their popular base. It may also evidence Sandinista success in reducing the erosion of their own support by altering unpopular policies.

Success is indisputable among the Miskito Indians of the Atlantic Coast, who revolted at the beginning of the decade against the new regime's efforts to impose strong central authority over an area long accustomed to neglect, however malign. By removing the comandante originally in charge of the Atlantic Coast, by facilitating reconstruction of villages along the Honduran border, by granting amnesty to opponents and opening negotiations over conditions of local autonomy, they seem to have somewhat reduced local hostility.

The Sandinistas themselves evince confidence in their ability to defeat the Contras without the aid of Eastern-bloc advisers and without acquiring additional weapons systems (such as combat aircraft) if the Contras must fight without U.S. aid and Honduran sanctuaries. The June 1986 Contadora draft treaty requires the withdrawal of foreign military advisers from all signatory states within 180 days of their acceptance of the treaty. The treaty also would require Nicaragua "not to acquire after the treaty comes into force any more military materiel, with the exception of replenishment supplies, ammunition and spare parts needed to keep existing materiel in operation." The treaty provides as well for an international corps of inspectors and a verification and control commission to monitor compliance. The government of Nicaragua has stated that it is prepared to sign. The governments of Honduras, Costa Rica, and El Salvador have rejected the draft, which has also been condemned by the Reagan administration.

Of course, if the treaty came into force, the Contras would be operating at a tremendous disadvantage vis-à-vis the Sandinista regime. Insurgents always operate with great handicaps. That is why most of them fail. But Somoza's overthrow does suggest that a truly broad-based popular rising in Central America can succeed when the United States plays an essentially neutral role.

I see little prospect of such a rising, unless the Sandinistas suddenly lurch self-destructively toward a collectivist progam for radically altering Nicaraguan society. The Sandinistas too seem confident that they have a winning formula for consolidating a regime in which, like Mexico's revolutionary elite and its successors, they will play a leading though not exclusive role in governance and management. Admittedly, their declared readiness to sign the draft treaty may be insincere, a mere gesture made safe by foreknowledge of the draft's rejection by the other necessary parties. But there is nothing to prevent us from testing their sincerity by urging our Central American dependencies to accept the treaty or something close to it. There is nothing, that is, other than an insensate desire to liquidate the present government of Nicaragua.

If I am right in believing that Nicaragua is prepared to practice nonintervention in its neighbors' affairs and strategic neutrality vis-à-vis the United States and the USSR in return for U.S. tolerance, the strategic argument for United States intervention, direct or indirect, loses the rationale attributed to it by Professor van den Haag. As he stands on the burning deck of his sinking polemical vessel, he may now, at the penultimate moment, find some alternative way at least of appearing to be afloat. I do hope that our last view will not be of him punting along in a little boat marked "credibility," the not–unfamiliar refuge of those who have run out of serious arguments. I prefer to believe he will see how peculiarly frail that claim would be in this instance where every major Latin American state opposes the Reagan administration's Nicaragua policy and opinion in our European allies varies from hostility to indifference. Nicaragua is another one of those peculiarly American obsessions.

Although initially he seemed indifferent to the human rights dimension of the administration's policy, during our second exchange Professor van den Haag declared that it needed to be taken into account. On that point we agree. So I turn to it now.

## The Moral Issue

Use of a separate subhead is designed solely for the reader's convenience, not to indulge Professor van den Haag's view that moral questions are largely, perhaps entirely, distinct from strategic ones. Whatever may be true of other nations, for the United States the two are, I believe, unalterably and intimately linked. Any political leader who loses sight of that fact is doomed to subvert the national interest.

In a democracy, leaders are agents, not principals. As agents, they must make their principals' definition of the national interest their own. Serving as they do a people with a profoundly moral self-image who demand acts confirming that image, just as they demand security and wealth, these agents cannot in good conscience employ means or pursue ends uninformed by conventional moral feeling.

Any democratic people, moreover, regard the preservation of democratic institutions and of the rule of law as a primary, probably as the preeminent, goal of foreign policy. We have discovered through the medium of Watergate and now Irangate that efforts by our leaders to secure problematic objectives by squalid means without broad public support lead ineluctably to the circumvention of law and the consequent erosion of those institutional balances and habits of self-restraint on the part of high officials that are essential to the preservation of a democratic polity.

Just as he found no disturbing complexity to analyze and assess in what he took to be the realm of strategy, Professor van den Haag finds agreeable simplicity in the moral realm. "No doubt," he concedes, "the Contras themselves too engage in acts of cruelty." But such acts, he adds dismissively, "are characteristic of civil wars." The decisive moral point, according to him, is that "Somoza's regime was mild, compared to the Sandinista regime [and] the Sandinistas will be far worse than the Contras are likely to be."

In the course of our second exchange I explained at length just why I was unable to believe the second of those two propositions. My skepticism, as I hope the reader will recall, stems in part from the character of the Contras, particularly from the prominent role former members of the National Guard have played in their armed contingents. It stems as well from appreciation of the frightful aftermath of anti-leftist and U.S.-supported takeovers in Chile and Guatemala. Since 1954 a white terror has enveloped the latter; its people have writhed under the rule of a civil-military coalition that in this decade alone has butchered tens of thousands of presumed opponents. The third source of skepticism is my judgment that the Sandinista leadership is neither fanatically doctrinaire nor furiously vengeful.

Had they been consumed by a desire for revenge, it seems to me that they would have followed the Cuban precedent and executed large numbers of captured members of the Guard. The Inter-American Commission on Human Rights sedulously investigated allegations that had in fact occurred and found them baseless. In its second report on the condition of human rights in Nicaragua (the first described conditions during Somoza's last stand), the commission concluded without dissent that it took the Sandinistas about two weeks, after Somoza's flight and the collapse of organized opposition, to reestablish central authority, that during that brief interregnum acts of vengeance were perpetrated by revolutionaries in violation of rules of combat laid down by the anti-Somoza leadership (and perfectly apolitical people may well have used the occasion to settle private scores), but that following the restoration of order, the new regime attempted in good faith, and in general successfully, to bring an end to the violence.

Since I treat the commission's reports as an important and reliable source of information, and since neither Professor van den Haag nor the reader may be entirely familiar with those features of the institution that lend it high credibility, before proceeding I should say a few words about them. Founded in 1959, the commission is a "principal organ" of the Organization of American States. The seven members of the commission are nominated by governments and elected by the member states of the OAS to four-year terms. They are usually distinguished jurists and not infrequently have held, or at the time of their election are holding, senior administrative, diplomatic, or judicial positions in their respective countries. As one would expect, given these electoral procedures and personal profiles, the ideology of members varies from liberal (in a minority of cases) to extremely conservative.

As the Sandinistas' treatment of the Guard belies the claim that they are remarkably ferocious, so their response to the vicissitudes of post-Somoza consolidation seems inconsistent with, or at least raises considerable doubt about, the charge that they are driven by ideological compulsion to press Nicaraguan society into a totalitarian mold. I have already called attention to revision in their approach to land reform and administration of the Atlantic Coast, as well as noting their effort to maintain a private manufacturing and commercial sector, albeit one not threatening the regime's political dominance. These signs of flexibility and ideological eclecticism in pursuit of social reform, enhanced national autonomy, and regime consolidation may be nothing more than a Machiavellian response to the threat posed by the United States and domestic opponents. Professor van den Haag has plenty of company in believing that, if the threat vanishes, so too will every element of pluralism in Nicaraguan society.

Unlike my colleague, I have never pretended that the available evidence permits a confident judgment about Sandinista intentions, assuming a single set of intentions can be imputed to people marked by not–trivial differences in education and organizational origins. Whatever millenarian visions may lurk in the furthest recesses of their hearts (a fact concerning which no one can claim clairvoyance), history and geography, I have argued, constitute formidable barriers to the establishment by the Sandinista party of a totalitarian and collectivist system. To the end of strengthening those barriers, I have proposed strategies of what might be called peaceful penetration backed by economic carrots and sticks and coordinated with leading Latin American and European states. Rather than addressing this option, Professor van den Haag prefers to label it "appeasement."

Any objective effort to envision the trajectory of a consolidated Sandinista-dominated regime must take account not only of arguable similarities between contemporary Nicaragua and the first phase of Cuba's revolutionary era but also of their differences. Within three years of Batista's flight, Castro had ripped off what now appears to have been a mask of respect for pluralism and purged all nonconforming elements in governmental and private institutions. Within six years he had launched those experiments in extreme egalitarianism—attempting virtually to exterminate market incentives in the process of creating "a new socialist man"—that helped, along with the flight of the upper classes and the U.S. economic blockade, to cripple the country's economy. Seven years into the post-Somoza era, Nicaragua retains important elements of pluralism and, even in the midst of wartime stringency, considerable private enterprise, above all in the agricultural and small commercial sectors. The Catholic Church endures as a powerful national force. Although denied access to the mass media, it is able through its broad clerical network to disseminate statements of opposition to government policies. While the Sandinistas monopolize television, about 30 radio stations remain in private hands. Saninista party stalwarts dominate the National Assembly, but representatives of the six opposition parties use the Assembly as a forum for expressing harsh criticism of government action. In April 1986, when a cluster of private groups in the United States organized a conference on the then-draft Nicaraguan Constitution, opposition politicians appeared beside a delegation led by the country's vicepresident and delivered a stinging critique.

The private *Comision Permanente de Derechos Humanos* continues to compile human rights complaints and to disseminate critical reports both in Nicaragua and abroad. Independent jurists continue to serve in the regular court system. When I last visited Nicaragua, in December 1986, opposition lawyers said that the regular judicial system continues to evidence a considerable degree of independence. (At least temporarily, however, it has lost jurisdiction over cases involving persons charged with serious violations of laws relating to national security. Those cases are heard by special tribunals. Although defendants before these tribunals are allowed counsel of their choice, the procedures are summary and the tribunal members are selected under procedures that effectively preclude impartiality.)

The compass of this colloquy is too narrow to permit an elaborate recounting of the present human rights situation. Americas Watch—the most careful, impartial, and well staffed of the various private organizations monitoring developments in Nicaragua—has issued a series of reports that, taken together, provide a richly detailed portrait readily available to anyone who does not want to take my or anyone else's summaries on faith. Some of those details are the subject of bitter dispute particularly between Americas Watch and the Reagan administration. But if we take only the facts I have enumerated, facts not susceptible to doubt, one must conclude that Nicaragua's trajectory differs significantly from the one followed by Cuba during its early postrevolutionary phase. The external threat does not offer a convincing explanation of that difference since it was hardly less intense in the Cuban case. The Bay of Pigs legions were Cuba's Contras. If the conclusion of the Cuban missile crisis signaled the temporary end to the threat of invasion, it certainly did not terminate efforts by the United States to overthrow the regime by all other means, including the assassination of Fidel Castro.

Of course, the comparative merit of the Cuban and Nicaraguan regimes is relevant at this point only to the extent it casts some light on the issue of whether, as Professor van den Haag wills himself to believe, "the Sandinistas will be far worse than the Contras are likely to be." His conviction about the relative benignity of Somoza reenforces his ideologically fired compulsion to believe in the relative merits of the Contras, Somocistas having played a considerable role in their creation.

I do not know why he believes that "Somoza's regime was mild, compared to the Sandinista regime." I do not know, because he has yet to tell me. Until the last two years of the family's regime, formally inaugurated following the presidential election of 1936 but effectively in place from the time of Augusto Sandino's assassination two years earlier, it tolerated an opposition consisting of other elite families, many of which periodically collaborated in the Somoza spoils system and all of which accepted—reluctantly or otherwise—the central rule of the political game: Elections could come and go; the Somozas would remain. For over 40 years, the National Guard (a private army answerable only to the family), the family's conspicuously close ties to the United States, and occasional exemplary cruelties sufficed to deter any serious challenge from other members of the upper classes. Any attempt to break out of the system would, moreover, have required mobilization of peasants and workers. Their continued passivity was in the common class interest of the regime and its opponents.

The last of the Somozas to rule, Anastasio, was irrational only in his greed. As long as opponents played the game, they helped legitimate it. This compensated for whatever nuisance they caused by calling attention in the National Assembly or the pages of *La Prensa*, the newspaper owned by the opposition leader Pedro Chamorro, to some conspicuous peculation of the president or some sadistic delinquency of his Guard.

If we compare the condition of human rights in Nicaragua during the years when the regime stood unchallenged with conditions today, and particularly if we look only at freedom of speech and press and numbers of people in detention, reference to Somoza's regime as relatively mild is not unreasonable. What is unreasonable is the comparison. The Sandinistas assumed power in the midst of a new era, an era marked by the broadening of political consciousness and the intensification of social unrest. When Anastasio Somoza felt the architectonic plates of society shifting beneath him, like fellow oligarchs and officers in El Salvador and Guatemala, he adapted by stepping up the level of repression. The only meaningful comparison is between Somoza and the Sandinistas *under stress*.

Two reports of the Inter-American Commission on Human Rights—one describing conditions in Nicaragua during the first stage of the uprising against Somoza, the other describing conditions in Nicaragua a year and a half after the Sandinistas' assumption of power—implicitly make that comparison and in the process leave Professor van den Haag's claim looking rather tattered. The report on Somoza, based in part on an on-site observation of conditions in the fall of 1979, is probably the most damning ever issued by an official body in the human rights field. It found his Guard guilty of murder and torture on a massive scale, and as a way of expressing collective belief that grave violations of the most fundamental human rights would continue as long as Somoza remained in power, it took the unprecedented step of formulating no ameliorative recommendations for the regime to consider.

Also based in significant measure on direct observation, the commission's report on postrevolutionary Nicaragua criticized restraints on freedom of speech and association, a failure of due process in the trial of members of the National Guard, and intense overcrowding in centers of detention. But, as I noted above, it found no basis for allegations of regime-sponsored torture and execution. On the contrary, it concluded that the new government was making a good faith effort to prevent abuses.

Having revisited the country twice since then and studied the reports of responsible journalists and various human rights organizations, I believe that, despite a sharp escalation of threats to the regime's survival, it has not followed the Somoza precedent, or the precedents established by the military establishments of El Salvador and Guatemala, of using mass murder, mutilation, disappearance, and unconstrained torture to suppress insurgents. There are confirmed instances of delinquencies committed by Sandinista troops or police agents. What distinguishes the government in Managua from its counterparts in San Salvador and Guatemala City, and from the Contras, is its willingness to apply sanctions, including imprisonment, against at least some delinquent members of its security services. Such sanctions were and remain inconceivable in its neighbors, as they were inconceivable in Argentina and Uruguay before the restoration of civilian governments. They were inconceivable because the "abuses" were not aberrations but rather the application of means endorsed by officials standing at the apex of effective authority. There are confirmed cases of murder and mutilation of civilians perpetrated by Contra units. The Contras have failed to adduce a single instance in which sanctions have been applied to the responsible parties. Moreover, the pattern of abuses strongly suggests a policy of assassinating supporters of the regime. Such a policy would be at worst an overexuberant application of the guidelines written for the main Contra force, the FDN, by an operative of the Central Intelligence Agency. And it is perfectly consistent with the behavior of National Guard units during the insurrection.

Lest Professor van den Haag or any other reader lose sight of the fact, such comparisons as I have made favorable to the Sandinista regime do not constitute a veiled claim that it has a "democratic" vocation in the Western sense of the word. On the basis of its evolution to date and the ideological background of its leading figures, I do not doubt its intention to retain decisive power over foreign and domestic policy. But as the Mexican regime has demonstrated, that intention is compatible with better than average levels of human rights for the general population if the regime is not determined to collectivize the economy and monopolize the social and cultural spheres. The Mexican experience also suggests, however, that if the Sandinistas are left free to achieve their objectives in the fields of education and health, they will ultimately produce demands for the true democratization of political life.

No government in our time is going to be so consistently successful or lucky in managing the economy and massaging the social conflicts immanent in every society as to satisfy indefinitely a literate, healthy, and politically alert population. Neither indoctrination nor the threat of Soviet intervention sufficed in Hungary and Czechoslovakia to achieve indefinite toleration of one-party rule. Even the party elite did not remain firmly and uniformly committed to it. Thus, in carrying out its goals for societal improvement, the Sandinista regime will create conditions conducive to its reformation or the emergence of a new Contra movement, but in that case one able to mobilize broad popular support. In my judgment, isolation and external threats delay the day of reckoning.

Recognizing as I do the multiple uncertainties associated with imagining the trajectory of any society, I will nevertheless submit for Professor van den Haag's consideration the following provocative hypothesis: that Nicaragua under a consolidated Sandinista regime experiencing normal diplomatic and commercial relations with the United States is more likely than El Salvador, Honduras, or Guatemala, under their current regimes, to evolve into a society where the population enjoys human rights at a level approaching that found in the United States and other capitalist democracies. I refer to levels of human rights rather than democratic rights or simply "democracy," because the Reagan administration and its ideological outriders insist on equating democracy exclusively with elections in which parties compete, the electorate is protected from overt intimidation, and its ballots are counted accurately, rather than seeing these as *necessary but not sufficient conditions*.

What does not seem to interest Washington is whether the resulting government actually exercises effective authority or has any reasonable prospect of doing so. Despite recent elections in Guatemala, Honduras, and El Salvador, the power of decision over every important policy issue continues to rest in the cantonments of the armed forces. Guatemala's President Cerezo has been entirely candid on this score, claiming publicly to have no more than 30% of real political power. He has admitted that, as a consequence, he cannot control the armed forces, he cannot bring to justice officers guilty of mass murder, he cannot guarantee the security of reformist politicians, human rights activists, labor leaders, or, for that matter, anyone the armed forces are inclined to regard as subversive, and he cannot initiate the reforms in land tenure required to provide a minimum of economic and social security for the vast mass of the population and to initiate sustained and balanced growth in the national product.

American conservatives seem equally uninterested in the question of whether extreme social and economic inequality, expressing itself in the form of mass illiteracy, ill health, and awful economic insecurity, constitutionally disables a formally competitive political process from performing its theoretical functions of aggregating the majority's preferences and translating them into public policy. If the media are monopolized by a few wealthy families that collaborate to suppress facts and views hostile to their class interests, if the provision of minimal governmental services to the immiserized population of barrios and villages is conditioned on collective voting for the traditional parties of the upper classes, if illiterates are denied the right to vote and government devotes so small a percentage of its potential revenues to education that illiteracy is perpetuated, if the principal parties consciously refrain from programmatic competition for the votes of the lower classes—if all these conditions exist, and they do to varying degrees in many Latin American countries, is it not somewhat disingenuous to refer to such political orders, in discourse among North Americans and Western Europeans, as "democratic"?

Citizens of the advanced capitalist democracies instinctively connect the procedures of democracy with the reality of social justice—that is, with real equality before the law, considerable equality of economic opportunity, and a safety net above absolute destitution. The image the word evokes in their minds does not correspond to present or foreseeable conditions in Honduras, El Salvador, and Guatemala.

Conservative intellectuals know this to be the case. I would like to see them address the resulting moral issues with somewhat greater candor.

The story is told of Montaigne, on a visit to a friend who happened to be head of the Inquisition in that part of France, being taken to the burning of an accused heretic. Afterwards, on the ride back to his host's castle, Montaigne seemed unusually pensive. "Of what are you thinking?" the friend is supposed to have asked. "I am thinking," replied Montaigne, "that you must value your opinions highly to roast people for them." Perhaps it is just because of some inchoate sense within the American body politic that we have organized, directed, and financed war in Nicaragua on no firmer basis than the ideologically fortified opinions (obsessions really) of a handful of people, that the most popular president since Franklin Delano Roosevelt (prior to Irangate), exploiting the vast propaganda resources of the national government and the organized Right, has failed to marshal broad public support for this war. That failure reinforces confidence in the good sense and the good heart of my fellow citizens.

CHAPTER 6

# Reality, Ideology, and Delusion

## ERNEST VAN DEN HAAG

Professor Farer writes: "One's position on any particular foreign policy issue is deeply influenced, I believe, by some sort of moral or aesthetic reflex, a finally unanalyzable preference for certain groups over others and for certain social and political arrangements."

Of course, I do have such preferences—some analyzable, some not—just as does my friend Tom Farer. But there is a difference between us about the difference these preferences make, or should make. Professor Farer thinks they are decisive or, at least, important in foreign policy matters. I think they are irrelevant. I feel that my preference or, generally, the American preference for any "group and for certain social and political arrangements" should not determine American support or opposition to that group. Our position should depend on the group's foreign policy. Only if its "social and political arrangements" lead the group to support American security interests should it be supported by us. If the group, whatever its domestic arrangements, is hostile to American security interests or threatens them, we should oppose it. It may be the case—indeed, it is likely—that its domestic arrangements will lead the group to be friendly or hostile to the United States, but it needn't be so. A democracy may oppose American interests at times, and, more often, a dictatorship may well support the United States. The dictator's enemies may appeal to our democratic sympathies. But we should not oppose the dictator if he supports our foreign policy interests.

I believe we should support dictatorships that support us, particularly in the long run, as well as democracies that do, not because we like or dislike either domestic arrangement but because we have interests in common, e.g., opposition to a common enemy. This justified our support of Stalin against Hitler (although we were overenthusiastic and insisted that, since he was attacked by Hitler, he must be a nice man, and communism must be superior to nazism). Our support was reasonable, i.e., in our interest, although it should have been more qualified. Similarly, we should always support anyone who is with us against our greatest threat, currently the Soviet Union. We may support the Chinese, the Mujahedeen in Afghanistan, the Contras in Nicaragua, Savimbi in Angola, dictators in Zaire or Kenya, or workers in Poland because it is in our interest to support those likely to decrease, or to prevent the increase of, Soviet power. If they are democratic, so much the better. But this is not a *conditio sine qua non*, nor is it sufficient.

To come back to international law, which intrigues or obsesses Professor Farer far beyond the role it does, and can, play in any reasonable analysis of foreign policy, he writes that the United States "cut and ran" when the International Court of Justice decided it had jurisdiction in the Nicaragua case. He is right. I have never understood why, in the first place, we tried to convince the Court that it did not have jurisdiction, instead of simply ignoring it and stating that we did not think it had jurisdiction to decide whether it did. The outcome was predictable, and no purpose was served—other than securing honoraria for lawyers—in placing the United States in a no-win situation. We should never have participated in the proceedings. Not that our case for the Court's incompetence was not good. I think we were right. But we should have known (actually we did) that the Court would decide against us by pretending it had jurisdiction in a case in which it didn't. Score one against the state department, which, unfortunately still is lousy with more or less frustrated lawyers who think foreign policy is about law and issues are decided by courts and that something called a court should never be ignored.* Foreign policy is about power and issues are decided by power, not by laws and courts.

Professor Farer regards the International Court of Justice as "impartial." I don't. The majority of members are elected or nominated by anti-American states. The Court's decisions reflect no less.†

Professor Farer suggests that he "could not tell" whether I agreed with his view that "the senior officials who . . . implement foreign policy are influenced . . . [by] what they take to be international law." Sorry he could not tell. I think they are. Unfortunately.

*The "International Court of Justice" has the trappings of a court, but, lacking compulsory jurisdiction and enforcement power, it is, at best, a group of grandiloquent lawyers willing to arbitrate what the nations submit to it. They can do nothing about anything not submitted to them by all participants. Verdicts not accepted by any party are not enforced.

†A footnote may not be amiss here. Some time ago Liberia and Ethiopia sued South Africa before the International Court of Justice, demanding that it evacuate Southwest Africa (now called Namibia), a former German colony which South Africa had occupied after World War I (an occupation that later became a mandate bestowed by the League of Nations). The lawsuit was—surprise—financed by the United States, and plaintiff's lawyers were American. There was no legal basis for the suit. I appeared as an expert witness for South Africa and testified to that effect. *Mirabile dictu*, South Africa won. What happened thereafter? The composition of the Court changed, the suit was brought once more under some pretext, and this time South Africa lost. The mandate was declared invalid, the occupation illegal. South Africa, of course, ignored the decision, and is still occupying Namibia. There are negotiations to end this occupation—again under American sponsorship. (No one has ever justified the American involvement.) But the court's verdict plays no role. The negotiations largely have to do with the presence of Cuban troops in Angola. The Communist government of Angola cannot do without these mercenaries, as everybody (except, of course, our state department experts) knows. Hence, they cannot be negotiated away and South Africa will stay in Namibia, at least as long as Angola has a pro-Soviet government.

What has all this to do with (1) international law, (2) the International Court of Justice? You guessed it: nothing. So with any halfway serious international problem.

Indeed, this is a major complaint against our state department, which, under the influence of its superabundant lawyers, persistently confuses foreign policy with a series of lawsuits, strategic interests with legal arguments. Instead of protecting American interests and power, the department worries about an international law that, I have shown, exists only in the minds of state department lawyers and their supporters such as my errant friend. An episode* illustrates the point:

When Somalia switched to our side, motivated largely by fear of, and hostility to, Ethiopia, which had obtained Soviet backing, we refused to support Somalia's attempt to take the Ogaden from Ethiopia. The area is inhabited by ethnic Somalis. Soviet military aid, Cuban troops, and our refusal to support our new friends enabled Ethiopia to resist successfully. The refusal of U.S. support was justified by the then-secretary of state, Cyrus Vance: "Although our agreement in principle to provide defensive arms to Somalia still stood, their involvement in the Ogaden prevented its implementation.... We also would not approve transfers to Somalia of U.S.-manufactured arms in the hands of Third World countries while Somalia was involved in Ogaden."† To a further appeal from Somalia, Vance responded: "As long as Somalia continued its invasion of Ethiopia.... we had to direct our efforts to limiting the conflict and getting Somalia out of the Ogaden so we could provide assistance without serious damage to our African policies."‡ In effect, Vance supported the Ethiopians and the Soviets for the sake of principles of international legality that have been enforced nowhere, at no time, and certainly were never taken seriously by either the Soviet Union or Ethiopia. Foreign policy and American interests were replaced by legal principles.

*I take the following from an essay, "The Busyness of American Foreign Policy," which I published in *Foreign Affairs* (Fall 1985).
†Cyrus Vance, *Hard Choices*, Simon and Schuster, New York, 1983, p. 73.
‡Ibid., p. 74.

Let me reiterate my view here as clearly as I can. Contrary to what Professor Farer implies, I believe, as he does, that adherence to customary, or agreed-on, norms of international behavior, and to treaty norms, can be quite useful—provided that that adherence is widely enough shared and not unilateral, as it has been in our relations with the Soviet Union, its allies, satellites, and would-be satellites. Such adherence is not good (or bad) *per se*. Its usefulness depends on reciprocity. To persist in it when others do not puts us at a disadvantage. And where the cost to us of adhering is greater than the cost of not adhering, we should not persist just to please those who confuse foreign policy with legal jousting. In practice—a fact Professor Farer refuses to recognize—powers other than the United States adhere to their interests, not to international law; they find their interests advanced by adherence to international law only when (1) their actions, by accident, conform to it (in which case international law may help propagandists: the opponent is shown to violate it and Professor Farer is impressed), or (2) the issue is so minor that adherence to international law is well worth (in terms of public relations) the minor sacrifice it may require. However, international law does not influence, let alone decide, major conflicts. Diplomacy (negotiation) and power do. Legal argument is used only to make the negotiated decision or the decision made by naked power look nice. International law at best is cosmetic. (It is no accident that in every war the loser is shown to have been legally wrong.)

Let me now draw attention to the unreality of Professor Farer's whole mode of argument. Fifty years ago we were confronted with Nazi Germany, which wanted to conquer the world, international law be damned. We resisted successfully by force. No international law, court, or association was of any help. We allied ourselves with those who feared Hitler and resisted, or attacked, him wherever we could, finally defeating Nazi Germany and executing its leaders by means of a pseudolegal proceeding (for which there was no basis in any law other than the *fiat* of the victors\*). I think we did the right thing to protect American interests, and the interests of mankind and we executed evil men, who deserved no less.

We are now confronted with a similar situation, the prospective enemy being the Soviet Union instead of Nazi Germany. There are some very major differences. Unlike the Nazis, the Soviets know that they cannot make further major conquests without confronting the United States. They do not feel inclined to risk that confrontation. They will not be so inclined as long as we remain strong enough and resolute enough to make the cost prohibitive for them. International law remains at best a side issue. The Soviets will use it when it favors them, ignore it when it does not. So should we. What protects us is readiness, not law: *Si vis pacem para bellum* (if you want peace be prepared for war), as the Romans, who invented international law, instructed the world.

The Soviets will continue to try to expand by proxy without risking major confrontations. Nicaragua is a case in point. Our task is to prevent such expansion by supporting any native resistance we can find and organize. International law? I don't think the Cubans who are in Nicaragua, or the Soviets, or the Sandinistas, who support the Communists in El Salvador, are interested. Why should we be?

Professor Farer thinks our interests are not served if by disregarding international law we diminish the ''predictability of interactions.'' I think international law does little to increase it. We can predict the behavior of the Soviet Union and that of the Sandinistas best, not by relying on international law but by studying the dy-

---

\*There was no legal basis for the charge of waging aggressive war and for the charge of committing crimes against humanity. There was for the charge of violating the laws and customs of war. Despite numerous wars and atrocities, no Nuremberg-like charges have ever been brought since World War II. Of course, one would have to defeat the Soviet Union, France, Egypt, or Indonesia before the trial—which then would become unnecessary. Although legally indefensible, in my opinion Nuremberg was a political and propaganda success and may be justifiable in emotional terms as well.

namics of communism, to which international law is not relevant. Did international law enable us to predict the invasion of Hungary? Czechoslovakia? Afghanistan? The Finlandization of Finland? The neutralization of Austria? The permanent occupation of East Germany and the refusal to let anyone but the Soviets govern East Berlin? Or the behavior of the Libyans, such as the invasion of Chad? And various acts of terrorism often aided and abetted by Libyan diplomats? Or the invasion of Timor by Indonesia? Just what is Professor Farer talking about?

Domestic law didn't do much to restrain Al Capone. Still, he was an exception—most of us are law-abiding. And the domestic law has teeth, which finally were used to imprison him. International law does not. And its subjects, particularly the Soviet Union and its allies, all behave like Al Capone. It is law-abiding nations that are the exception. Further, the international gangster governments are also supposed to be the policemen and judges who are expected to arrest and punish themselves. Could anything be more absurd?

Farer (more or less) attributes to me the idea that "treaties would have no place" in a world without international law wherefore "the arduous work of negotiating and ratifying them would be a waste of time." This is not my view. (Attacking straw men is easy but hardly instructive.) I contend that in international relations one cannot rely on treaties to bind parties or predict their actions. Yet one should negotiate them because the process may (1) clarify everybody's intentions and interests, (2) persuade our public opinion that we do what we can to settle conflicts peacefully, (3) help both parties to discover compromises that may be more satisfactory than conflict. If the general situation does not change, and the aims of both parties are compatible with peaceful relations, treaties may even (4) settle some conflicts at least temporarily (but everything is temporary) and make the behavior of both parties more predictable than otherwise, just as Professor Farer contends.

His error is to believe that treaties always will have that effect. They sometimes do. Whether or not they do does not depend on international law but on whether the power relations underlying the treaties remain unchanged. If they do, treaties can be helpful. The treaties between Portugal and England have served well for centuries. But if the power situation or the national interests of either party change, treaties become ineffective and belief in treaties can become a snare and a delusion. Professor Farer thinks treaties have an autonomous role to play according to legal rules. I regard this as a dangerous kind of wishful thinking.

Farer goes out of his way to demonstrate his self-deception by repeatedly offering invalid analogies to domestic law. He simply ignores the difference. Domestic law is enforceable: Courts interpret it, police enforce it. Interpretation and adherence is not simply left to the parties. International law, in contrast, is at most a series of customs and agreements, or treaties, which are not subject to binding interpretations and cannot be enforced. They are adhered to when the parties find it convenient, not when they do not. Hence, the analogy to domestic law is misleading rather than enlightening.

So are the particulars. Professor Farer writes: "Like participants in domestic legal systems, states will construe treaty provisions...in a manner most favorable to themselves but...they will...recognize, first,...[that other states may imitate them]" and, second, that "they may undermine an agreement or customary rule that is in general beneficial." Spoken like a lawyer. Precedents are everything. But states do not give a damn about precedents (although their law departments trot them out when helpful for propaganda purposes) or about encouraging others. Policy makers ignore this sort of thing (except, possibly, in our state department). When invading Hungary the Soviet Union did not ask: Will this encourage other invasions? Set a precedent? Encourage the Hungarians to invade us? Encourage the Americans to invade Cuba? Violate treaty obligations? Will our invasion injure generally beneficial customary rules of conduct? What the Soviets ask is quite different, to wit: What is the cost (not including Mr. Farer's legal worries), the actual military and political cost? Does the benefit warrant it? What are the alternatives? Correctly, from its viewpoint, the Soviet Union invaded Hungary. In a different power situation it might not have dared. International law? Be serious. So with Afghanistan. International law? Treaties? They can set effective rules only to the extent the *status quo* is accepted by everybody. When Hungary tried to change its domestic order in ways that the Soviet Union thought might lead to its actual independence, the Soviets intervened. Predictably—if, unlike Professor Farer, you base predictions on experience rather than on international law.

We intervened less directly and less brutally in Nicaragua, by helping the Contras, not because we mind Nicaragua's domestic order—although we stupidly helped Nicaraguans to get rid of Somoza in the naïve hope that his Sandinista opponents were humanitarians democrats—but because it has become clear that the Sandinistas act as a Soviet proxy and will try to help Cuba and the Soviet Union to dominate Central America, and thereby to endanger the U.S. position in the hemisphere.

Sometimes Professor Farer admits what he elsewhere strenuously denies. We do not invade Canada, he avers. "Is law the explanation of our restraint? Not entirely. Not even primarily, I suppose." He supposes right. There is a simple reason for not invading Canada. (1) It does not threaten us in any way. (2) Canada supports our foreign policy in all important respects. (3) The United States would not benefit in any way if it conquered Canada.*

The Soviets "do not escort their fishing fleets with warships," Professor Farer triumphantly tells us, but instead buy fishing licenses. This, according to my deluded friend, shows their reverence for treaties and customs. It merely shows that fishing licenses

---

*Professor Farer once more betrays his economic naïveté when he depicts Canada's "great lode of natural resources" as an enticement for us to conquer it. Why would these natural resources be cheaper, more available, or, somehow, more beneficial to us if Canada were to become an American state? The theory of mercantilism, on which such ideas are based, has long been discredited among economists, if not among lawyers.

are cheaper. As is arbitration in many cases. One uses force only when it is cheaper and the risk–reward ratio is favorable.

Back to Nicaragua. "The United States in supporting the Contras is violating international law," Professor Farer states, "and that is a sufficient reason for terminating support." Not so. (1) Our support does not violate international law. (2) Regardless, I don't see why we should be bound by an international law that the Soviet Union violates with impunity whenever convenient. We need not unilaterally disarm our foreign policy. (3) For this reason, even if support of the Contras upsets international lawyers—or some of them—that is no reason for terminating it.

As for the "persuasive reasons" Farer demands for supporting the Contras, here are a few.

Morally we have an interest in avoiding a totalitarian dictatorship in Central America. We made a mistake in allowing its institution—actually helping it—in Cuba. We need not repeat it. We have a moral duty to protect at least our neighbors against it, particularly after we abetted (against international law?) the overthrow of Somoza.

More important, we have a strategic interest in preventing any additional Soviet outposts from being established in our neighborhood. Indeed, we have a strategic interest in containing Soviet power, preventing its further expansion wherever feasible at reasonable cost. That is why we should help Savimbi in Angola, or the rebels in Mozambique, or Afghanistan, and certainly the Contras. By supporting them we hope to prevent the consolidation of a Soviet outpost on the American continent. I cannot think of anything more legitimate and more necessary to protect our interest. Let me note here that a more alert and effective foreign policy might have made our liberation of Grenada by direct military means unnecessary. We might have organized effective native opposition. It is not too late to do so in Nicaragua.

Some people are shocked at our having full diplomatic relations with Nicaragua and, at the same time, supporting the Contras, who fight the Sandinista government *manu militari* and would certainly like to overthrow it. I find nothing shocking about this. It is in the Nicaraguan interest and in our own to continue diplomatic relations. For the reasons mentioned it is also in our interest to support the Contras. The contradiction between these two interests and their pursuit is purely legal: We recognize the government yet try our best to get rid of it. This sort of thing happens often. The Soviets certainly continued to recognize the Hungarian government while succeeding in overthrowing it. We continued to recognize Somoza in Nicaragua while helping to overthrow him. We should pursue both policies—helping the Contras and having diplomatic relations with the Sandinistas—as long as we find both to be in our interest. The fact that they are legally inconsistent matters as much as any legal argument matters in foreign policy—that is, not at all.

Professor Farer attributes to me the view that "[Communist] ideology is a precise and unalterable determinant of policy," a view that "insofar as human rights are concerned, rests on no persuasive factual grounds." I don't hold that view. The testimony of Gulag residents notwithstanding, things can always get worse—or sometimes, better. Roman Catholic ideology certainly has changed from the Spanish Inquisition to current notions. Calvinists no longer burn people. Ideologies tend to pass from initial virulence to mellower phases—but it takes time, time in which human rights, if inconsistent with the ideology, may suffer. And ideologies may go through renewed virulence.

Many German Jews, sharing Mr. Farer's ideas, decided Hitler would not actually practice his anti-Semitic ideology. It was not a precise and "unalterable determinant of policy." They remained in Germany and were "exterminated"—Hitler's anti-Semitism became more, not less, virulent in time. On the other hand, the Soviet ideology and the Soviet practice, terrible though it remains, are not quite as bad as they were in Stalin's time.

What are we to conclude? Ideology is not "unalterable." It may well change over time, becoming more, or less, "radical." It

is not a "precise determinant of policy"—ideologies themselves
seldom are precise. But ideology certainly is influential enough to
pay attention to. To find out what role it plays and to gauge an
appropriate reaction, we must look closely at what actually happens
in the country the government of which professes the ideology. If
what they are doing fits with the ideology, and with previous historical experiences, ideology is a good guide to the future.

In the case of Nicaragua, the development is quite near that of
a Communist state in Cuba, which, in turn, paralleled similar developments in East Germany, Romania, or Yemen. Until Castro
himself avowed that he had been a Communist all along, Professor
Farer's friends and, not least, *The New York Times* suggested that
anyone accusing him of introducing communism to Cuba was just a
hysterical red-baiter. To discount ideology and experience in
Nicaragua seems nothing less than frivolous wishful thinking,
where it is not deliberate deception.

The Soviet ideology outside Russia sometimes can be mod-
ified and mitigated in important, though not in decisive, respects.
Hungary shows as much. Czechoslovakia shows that such reforms
can easily fail. Note that mitigations of the Hungarian kind have
never been undertaken in developing countries. There Soviet ideology never is less virulent than in the Soviet Union itself.

China is the exception. But this was the result of Mao's disastrous policies, his timely death, and, not least, China's military and
economic independence of the Soviet Union and its satellites. No
such luck in Nicaragua. True, as Professor Farer points out, Albania, though following the Soviet model, is independent of, even
hostile to, the Soviet Union. So what? Some tyrannies don't like to
be tyrannized over, and may be able to do without Soviet tutelage.
But that is not often the case and certainly not at all in Central
America. Albania is clearly an exception. As is Yugoslavia, which
became nonaligned. It never was dependent on the Soviet Union, as
other Communist regimes, including Cuba and Nicaragua, are.

I don't know what to make of Professor Farer's implicit denial that his liberal friends were just as sanguine about Cuba when Castro took power as he is now about Nicaragua. Yes, it is the old liberal song again. I'm astonished that Professor Farer chants it with so little embarrassment. Experience teaches, but not everyone is willing or able to learn from it. Farer does not improve matters by asserting that, somehow, the fault for Communist expansion is to be laid at the door of those who, "fearing the spear of revolution, dispatched guns and cash to Latin America and set up counter-revolutionary schools for Latin scoundrels."* I don't think these schools brought communism to Cuba or, now, to Nicaragua. In both cases the Communists were supported by American liberals, Mr. Farer's friends, who took the Communists' word for it that they had no intention to set up a dictatorship. They promptly did.

Despite its repetitive and comic elements, it is sad to see this same tragedy unfolding over and over: cunning Communists who dupe "useful idiots," as Lenin called them, into supporting them. The useful idiots never learn. And there always are new ones.† They over and over "have seen the future and it works." After the Soviet Union got too discredited for all but total fanatics, Mao's China (nobody but us "agrarian reformers" here, according to Professor Owen Lattimore) became the place. It was paradise. They got rid of capitalists, mosquitoes, syphilis, prostitution, and all other weaknesses that flesh is heir to. As that petard exploded in the face of those who planted it, Cuba became the new paradise. (Same thing: no prostitution, more literacy.) But any paradise always gets worn after 10 or 20 years—the truth leaks out: It was hell all along, not paradise. Professor Farer's friends have an uninterrupted record of having supported, admired, and apologized for the worst dictatorships of the century: the Soviet Union, China, Vietnam (somehow North Korea never cared to get their support), Cuba. Hitler

*Perhaps they are scoundrels, although we have but Farer's assertion. But they are *our* scoundrels. I'd rather bribe them than have them help the Communists.
†On this matter see Paul Hollander's excellent *The Political Pilgrims,* Oxford University Press, New York, 1981.

made the mistake of using rightist rather than leftist symbols. That made him unattractive to intellectuals attracted to leftist symbols as bees are to honey. Moreover, Hitler was overtly anti-Semitic (rather than covertly, as the Soviets are). Wherefore Mr. Farer's friends never supported Hitler—they confined their enthusiasm to his quondam ally, Stalin. Don't they ever get tired? Must we see a replay in and about Nicaragua? I guess we must.*

I believe we made a mistake in sending troops to Vietnam. The generous impulse to help the Vietnamese ward off their miserable fate under communism was noble. Their fate after the victory of the Communists has borne out the most dire predictions. Still, our intervention was a mistake. First, in execution. We should have helped the South Vietnamese military forces, not replaced them. Our handling of the conflict was exceedingly inept. Second, we went there having adopted the doctrine of "one world" or "collective security" or the "domino theory" (invented by Stalin's foreign minister Maxim Litvinov), which required that we defend wherever the Communists attack, even if the target does not warrant the cost of defense, lest other dominoes fall. This is a foolish doctrine for it gives the enemy the choice of the battlefield and would cause us to dissipate out resources by requiring us to engage in costly defense even of unrewarding positions. We should defend only what is important to us, and when the defense is cost effective.

The situation with Nicaragua differs from that in Vietnam. Nicaragua is not so far away a place as Vietnam is. It is the sort of place the Monroe Doctrine contemplated. It is not an advantageous battlefield for the Soviets. Not that I favor sending the marines. I do not believe that the benefits would match the costs—material, moral, political. I favor doing exactly what the Soviets do and what

---

*Lest I be misunderstood, Farer, unlike his friends, is too sophisticated to pretend that Nicaragua is paradise. He feels we should leave Nicaragua undisturbed because otherwise we might violate fantasies about international law, and, anyway, Nicaragua should not be important to us. The conclusion does not differ from that of his more naïve friends, although his argument is, well, more sophisticated.

we finally are learning to do. They support, directly and indirectly, the Sandinistas, who are instituting a Soviet-style dictatorship and are willing to do the Soviets' bidding. We should support those who favor democracy and oppose Soviet influence in Nicaragua, to wit, the Contras. A hundred million dollars a year probably will do it. This is far less than what the Soviets spend. It will be effective enough. And we can afford it better than they can. We cannot afford as readily to take all the costly measures we will have to take once the Soviets are fully established in Nicaragua and feel safe enough to threaten expansion into the neighborhood. They already have the biggest and best-equipped (Soviet-equipped, of course) army in all of Central America. Although they have a population less than 5% that of Mexico, they have a bigger army.

Professor Farer is perfectly right in his reiterated claim that the outcome of political developments is never certain. Thus, Che Guevara achieved but his own death when he tried to export the Cuban revolution to the rest of America. Of course, attempts don't always succeed. The Cubans and Soviets try, however. They may succeed sometimes. Politics does not deal with certainties. It deals with probabilities and sometimes only with possibilities. It seems quite probable that (1) the Sandinistas are trying to institute a Communist dictatorship in Nicaragua, more or less on the Soviet model. They are proceeding slowly and have not yet succeeded. But (2) they will succeed unless the Contras interfere. (3) Their regime will be allied to, and dependent on, Cuba and, directly and indirectly, the Soviet Union. It already is. (4) The activities of the Sandinista regime will be harmful not only to the Nicaraguan people but also to American foreign policy interests. (5) The cost of preventing Sandinista consolidation by means of the Contras is much lower than the cost of not preventing it. Prevention will mean that the Sandinistas will have to share power with the opposition formally and informally.

Professor Farer points out that Argentina and Brazil have moved toward democracy, as has Uruguay, and that the Chile–

Argentina conflict was peacefully resolved. These developments are most welcome. But we should not forget what preceded them. Democracy occurred in Argentina after the military dictatorship had shown its total incompetence by starting and losing the Falklands war. Communism is no danger, for the time being, in Argentina because the military dictatorship had destroyed it—not without torturing and killing many people who merely held left-wing views or were suspected of holding them, or, finally, displeased in some other way the uniformed gangsters who run the country. Nonetheless, in addition to killing innocents, these military gangsters got rid of their Communist colleagues.

A similar process prevented Uruguay from falling victim to the Communists (Tupomaras). Now the military dictatorship, having discredited itself by brutality and incompetence, is being replaced by a democratric regime. Chile still has the dictatorship that came to power by overthrowing the pro-Communist Allende government.* All signs are that it will be replaced by a democratic regime, as soon as the opposition can get together and the Communist danger subsides.

I wish I could believe with my friend Tom Farer that "experience has also discouraged both millenarian goals and doctrinaire economic nostrums." Experience does not play that role—else Nicaragua would never have happened after the Cuban experience, or Cuba after the Soviet experience. Professor Farer's naïveté would long have been shattered. The will to believe all too often overcomes experience. It has in his case.

Contrary to what Professor Farer thinks, I do not believe that the Sandinista "capacity to maintain resistance and inflict casualties can deter invasion" by the United States. Nor do the Sandinistas believe that. They are not quite so naive. They spend on the army

---

*The United States is accused, in left-wing mythology, of having organized that overthrow. I would gladly plead guilty, but I doubt that we played but a minor role. (Only in Guatemala did we play a major role in overthrowing the pro-Communist regime of President Arbenz.)

partly for domestic control purposes and partly because it may come in handy against their neighbors—provided the United States does not defend them. (That is quite possible if Professor Farer's friends win in Washington. Incidentally, is there any Communist country that does not spend exorbitantly on its army—even if the people literally starve?)

Professor Farer holds up, as a model for us to imitate with the Sandinistas, the settlement the Soviet Union made with Finland. He forgets that that settlement was preceded by an unprovoked war the Soviet Union waged (and nearly lost) against Finland. When Stalin realized that making Finland into a Soviet satellite and a Communist country, as he had originally intended, would cost far more resources than he could spare, and when the Finns, on the other hand, realized that neither the West nor Hitler, preoccupied with their own fights, could help Finland, Stalin compromised. He took part of Finland's territory (Carelia) but dropped demands that Finland become Communist (though Communists initially had to be included in the Finnish government) in exchange for ironclad guarantees that Finland's foreign policy would be pro-Soviet, or neutral. Finland had to disarm. But it remained a democracy. The reasons for not following that model, which Professor Farer recommends for our relations with the Sandinistas, are:

1. We have not been at war with Nicaragua; nor have we been nearly defeated, as the Soviets were. Hence, no peace settlement can be imposed on us or on the Nicaraguans.

2. What part of Nicaragua does Farer want to annex to the United States? Have the Sandinistas shown any inclination to let us have part of their country?

3. Before and after the Soviet aggression the Finns had a democratic government that (a) could be trusted to keep its word, and (b) had no intention of subverting its neighbors.

Nicaragua never had a democratic government. The current Sandinista dictatorship cannot be trusted. The United States should not be seen to betray the people of Nicaragua and Central America.

The Finns escaped the Communist embrace. Whereupon Farer tells us that if we leave the Nicaraguans to Communist mercies we follow the example of the Soviet–Finnish settlement.

Professor Farer is probably right in telling us that it is unlikely that Nicaragua will send troops to Angola, Abyssinia, or other Communist regimes, the way Cuba has. But I didn't foresee Cuba's action either—did Professor Farer? Had I predicted it, would he have called me a hysterical red-baiter? Anyway, the Sandinistas, when not deterred by their own weakness, may well send troops, etc., to Honduras or other Central American countries.

Incidentally, Professor Farer claims that, since Ethiopia and Angola "continue, in any event, to ship such goods as they have to the West," we need not worry. The Soviet Union too ships what it can to the West, and Cuba would export to the United States if we'd let it. They want money to buy Western goods with. In what way does this make their regimes more appetizing or less dangerous?

"What," Professor Farer asks, "could Nicaragua add to the resources Cuba has...?" Little, to be sure, but it is a silly question. What would the Argentine generals expect the Falklands to add to Argentina? What, Mrs. Thatcher might have asked, is England losing in giving them up? The point is quite different. England would have been shown to yield to the military swagger of a third-rate dictatorship had it not resisted. The long-run moral and material cost was incalculable. The Argentine gangsters would have consolidated their regime and looked for new adventures. Allowing Nicaragua to fall to the Sandinistas altogether would indeed discredit United States resistance to communism, encourage the Communists in Central America, and give them a military base to be used against other Central American countries—even if they do not send troops to Angola. Castro does so to ingratiate himself with the Soviet Union and to deserve his subsidy. He has disappointed the Soviets by being unable to expand in Latin America and the Caribbean. Who knows what services the Sandinistas ultimately will perform for their masters. They don't lack the will, even if the opportunity has not yet arisen. It took Cuba quite a while too before it started exporting its conscripts.

Let me conclude this chapter with some general remarks about our foreign policy.

We are now hesitantly trying to contain Soviet expansion in some places by supporting indigenous forces willing to resist it. Relying on native forces is certainly politically more cost-effective than direct intervention. But trying to repel Soviet expansion in Nicaragua or Afghanistan is not enough. Not only should we support local resistance in Nicaragua, El Salvador, or Afghanistan; we should also retaliate for Soviet attempts at power expansion by increasing pressure on vulnerable Soviet spots elsewhere on the globe. The Soviets should not be allowed to choose local battlefields without fear of retaliation elsewhere. The response to Nicaragua should never be limited to Nicaragua. It should involve pressure, say, on the pro-Soviet regimes in Angola (by helping Savimbi), in Mozambique (by helping the antigovernment guerrillas), and in Ethiopia (by helping Somalia, Eritrea, and antigovernment Ethiopians).

Arguments against this policy, which, much too hesitantly, we have begun to follow, strike me as unconvincing. Usually they contend that these countries might be lured from Soviet dependence if we are nice to their governments. Yet their governments could not stay in power without Soviet help. Some African leaders may be displeased if we help native anti-Communists. But why should we grant them veto power as a gift? How do they deserve it?

Incidentally, why do we continue to debate whether the Contras or the Sandinistas are nicer, as though it mattered? The latter are pro-Soviet, the former are not. Do we need to know more?

The defects of our policies are not produced by theories of isolationism or interventionism, nor even by ideological factors, which account only for minor extravagances such as disinvestment in South Africa. We are dealing with fuzziness and institutional deficiencies.

The institutional trouble is that we have embassies for each country, and state department desks that tend to conceive of our policy toward, say, Ethiopia or Romania as a policy only toward either, and not as part of a global strategy. Assistant secretaries in charge of regions, such as Central America, supervise the desks. But the assistant secretary in charge of Central America is not expected to propose moves in southern Africa to make the Soviets pay for what happens in Nicaragua. And the assistant secretary for southern Africa would not like such proposals. He does not want his region to be used for global strategies. Nor do ambassadors. Our foreign policy is sectional at best, not global. The secretary of state, the president, and various planning boards are supposed to think globally. But the pull toward meeting regional problems on a regional basis seems to be strong enough to prevent global strategy from being practiced. Assistant secretaries regard regional settlements and treaties as feathers in their cap, regardless of global strategies.

Yet treaties to settle regional disputes are not necessarily in our interest. We are more interested—or should be—in imposing costs on Soviet expansion in any part of the globe by destabilizing regions currently under Soviet influence. We should not confine ourselves to local responses. It is only by retaliation that the Soviets may be discouraged. Here ideology and *realpolitik* converge quite nicely. Yet these specific policies have but a tenuous link to disputes about interventionism, isolationism, or ideology, which have become quite irrelevant.

Why are we so hesitant and ambivalent?

Foreign policy, conceived as the defense of specific American interests abroad and of American security, is still relatively new to the United States. Until the 20th century we scarcely had serious security concerns; indeed, alliances would have been "entangling." In the United States, foreign policy has long been perceived as the pursuit of lofty concerns—international peace, self-determination, democracy, human rights law—that are national ideals more than national interests.

Nuclear missiles have irrevocably changed the underlying reality. But our ideals and our foreign interests remain conflated. And many Americans still are under the impression that a benevolent deity has made sure that there is a just solution for every problem, a remedy for every wrong, which can be discovered by negotiations, based on goodwill and on American moral and legal ideals, self-evident enough to persuade all parties, once they are revealed by negotiators, preferably American.

Often, when American interests were involved, we have refused to see that at least indirect intervention could be useful and effective. Unless one of the parties was able to appeal to a democratic American constituency, it has been hard for the United States to intervene, directly or indirectly. Indeed, we seldom stress indirect intervention—yet that is what diplomacy ought to be all about. Often, the fact that none of the parties directly involved lived up to American ideals has blinded us to our interests. When we intervened nonetheless, we had to pretend that the party we supported was, after all, not just better than the party we opposed, but actually decent. Thus, when we decided that it was in our interest to support Stalin against his former ally, Hitler, we had to persuade ourselves that Stalin was not so bad and could be handled by our foreign-policy makers. We are still paying the price for this unjustifiable self-deception.

A realistic foreign policy would be guided by specifiable national interests and by the means we have, and are willing to use, to actually pursue them. It need not be inconsistent with principles of law and morality, but it should not confuse any principles with our national interests. History is not explained by moral or legal principles, although it is, after all, the result of past foreign policies.

Perhaps the American people have, as Professor Farer contends, a "profoundly moral self image"—although I cannot quite make out what that means. (I do not know of any nation that has a "profoundly immoral self-image.") Does it mean that we want our policies to be morally justifiable? Surely. Is there any nation that does not? The question is not: Should we be moral? But rather:

Which of many available policies is morally justifiable? Obviously, I think that support of the Contras is and Professor Farer does not. Insistence on "morality" will not clarify our disagreement. Stalin thought that killing kulaks (peasants who were insufficiently poor and suspected of opposing his confiscations) was morally justified, as did Hitler killing Jews.

Professor Farer neglects one point about morality. A democratic nation does not elect its government—its agent, as Professor Farer correctly says—to enact the various and inconsistent moral views of the voters. Our government is a fiduciary. Its task is to make it possible for the citizens to pursue happiness according to their own (not to the government's) morality. The government is to secure their life, their liberty, their property, and generally the conditions needed to pursue happiness. That, and that alone, is the government's task in foreign policy too. We do not elect the government to impose Professor Farer's morality, or mine, on anyone. As far as foreign relations are concerned, we elect the government to make sure that no foreign power will be able, directly or indirectly, to interfere with our independence, and ultimately to impose its morality on us by gaining the power to do so. That is why we fought Hitler and helped the Soviet Union to do so, although we were aware (at least I was) that it did not (and still does not) in Professor Farer's phrase "regard the preservation of democratic institutions and the rule of law" as its goal. We did not fight to impose this goal, which we cherish, on the Soviet Union. Actually, we allied ourselves to the Soviets under Stalin to counter the threat that came from the Germans under Hitler. Now the threat comes from the Soviet Union itself. Wherefore we may have to ally ourselves with, or to support, governments and movements that may not have much in common with us, other than fear of the Soviet Union. We must do what we did vis-à-vis Hitler. This is why we help dozens of African dictatorships as well as Asian and Near Eastern ones. We would be a little too lonely for comfort if we were to ally ourselves only to democratic states or movements. If that is what Professor Farer means by morality, I would be insulting the intelligence of our readers were I to spend time refuting such silliness.

But Professor Farer does not actually propose to isolate us. His morality is selective. He opposes alliance with, or support of, movements he regards as rightist, or insufficiently leftist, such as the Contras in Nicaragua. Against them he will let loose blasts of rhetoric telling about their cruelty and nastiness, incompatible with our democratic ideals. As for movements using leftist symbols, such as the Sandinistas, the motley opponents of the Chilean government of Augusto Pinochet, the Communists who fight the white government in South Africa, allied to and, in effect, dominating the ANC—well, boys will be boys. The ANC "comrades" in South Africa are in the habit of burning to death fellow blacks suspected of supporting the South African government or, at least, of not supporting the comrades. This is done by putting tires filled with gasoline around the necks of the suspects and slowly burning them. After all, it's done for a good cause, so Professor Farer's friends feel uncomfortable about it but do not make a fuss. Now, the alleged cruelties of the Contras, that is another matter. The Contras have not engaged in the refinements of the ANC—but, after all, the Contra cause is bad, isn't it? Opposing P. W. Botha excuses anything. Opposing Daniel Ortega nothing.

To my mind, things are simpler than Professor Farer would like. However dubious the pedigree of some of our allies, however much we disapprove of some of their actions, the autocratic or authoritarian governments we often had to support have proved amenable to a nonviolent transition to democracy. It happened in Greece, Spain, Portugal, and a number of Latin American countries. No such development has ever occurred once a country has fallen under the sway of the Communists. Therefore, we should make every effort to prevent communism where we can. In Nicaragua we must support the Contras. Elsewhere in Latin America we must oppose Communists and their proxies by supporting non-Communist governments.

Professor Farer admits that Castro "executed" (i.e., murdered) many opponents. (Did he oppose Castro at the beginning when his friends supported him?) He says the Sandinistas are not all that bad. Not yet. It takes them longer than it took Castro. But I would not bet on the future.* There is no reason to assume they will behave like democrats once they no longer are interested in swaying Professor Farer and his friends—once they have succeeded in getting rid of American assistance to the Contras.

Professor Farer speaks of a "white terror" unleashed in Guatemala, in which thousands of "presumed opponents" of the power holders were killed. (Apparently none were real opponents of the government; the leftist guerillas were only play-acting; they never killed anybody.) The term *white terror* was invented by the Bolshevists about 70 years ago to refer to the efforts—some cruel, some legitimate—of their opponents to fight them. "White terror" or not, I wish these anti-Bolshevists, whom we supported (albeit ineptly) over the opposition, of course, of the liberals, had won. The Russians would have been spared the Gulag. Forty million people killed by the Bolshevists (more than Hitler ever dreamt of, but, to be fair, the Communists had more time) would be alive.† The Baltic states, Hungary, Romania, Czechoslovakia, East Germany, Poland, Afghanistan—shall I go on?—would be free. Yet the liberals of that time, cloned now by Professor Farer and his friends, told us then that we were driving the Bolsheviks into becoming totalitarians. Were it not for us, they had a basically friendly, if not democratic, disposition. Anyway, they were morally superior to us. Red terror was invented by "red-baiters" or, anyway, was our fault. The liberals haven't changed their song. They just find new occasions and places to sing it. President Daniel Ortega, of

*It may be that Tom Farer, as a lawyer, is seduced by the admirable motto that every accused person is innocent until proven guilty. Good idea for criminal procedure. But not for foreign policy (or employment). In foreign policy you must prevent what you suspect will be harmful, foster what you hope will be helpful. You cannot wait for evidence beyond a reasonable doubt. Only historians and law professors, not foreign-policy makers, can afford to wait for totally conclusive proof. Policy makers must go on the best evidence available.
†See Robert Conquest, *The Red Terror,* Macmillan, New York, 1968.

Nicaragua, unlike Stalin, wears glasses and speaks Spanish. How, then, can we compare him to the Soviet tyrant, or to Castro, who has a beard? There is a sucker born every minute, and many who are not born to it seem to become suckers. Studying international law seems to help. (I don't know of any professor of international law who is not, shall we say, a liberal.)

"History and geography," Professor Farer intones, bar a totalitarian system in Nicaragua. He does not tell why "history and geography" were mute in Cuba. Of course, the Sandinistas can impose such a system—unless we prevent them. It is not "history and geography" but we who bar such a system in Nicaragua. We didn't do so in Cuba. We were lulled into passivity by Mr. Farer's friends.* Need we repeat the error?

Professor Farer thinks that what I would term appeasement— economic incentives—should be tried in Nicaragua. I know of no case where such incentives (or, for that matter, economic sanctions) have been effective in diverting a government from a totalitarian course. Russia itself is a good case in point. Moreover, we did plenty of economic favors for the Sandinistas before we knew what they were up to, as we did for Castro. To no avail. Why repeat a failed tactic? If Professor Farer refuses to learn from experience, must we all close our eyes?

Yes, as Farer declares, the Roman Catholic Church has retained influence in Nicaragua, and there are private radio stations.† Yet one bishop of the church has been exiled, foreign priests have been deported, a "popular" church independent of Rome and dependent on the Sandinistas has been created. The church retains influence because the government can't help it—not because it likes pluralism. The Pope, when he addressed the people of Nicaragua, was interrupted by organized Sandinista chanting of slogans. He was not treated that disrespectfully by the overtly Communist government of Poland. Freedom of the press has been abolished. *La*

---

*The Bay of Pigs was a belated and halfhearted attempt to repair the damage.
†However, the stations owned and operated by the church have been closed.

*Prensa*, the anti-Somoza newspaper, has been closed for excessive independence. Even Somoza left it alone for many years, until his own demise. The paper didn't survive the Sandinistas, although, according to Farer, they are so much nicer than Somoza. Opposition parties can "use the National Assembly for harsh criticism," Mr. Farer states. He neglects to mention that the "harsh criticism" cannot be published.

Perhaps the judiciary has not been altogether politicized, as Farer notes. Probably divorces and burglaries are handled as before the Sandinistas. But for whatever they decide is "political," there are special courts, which are as political as "people's courts" in Nazi Germany or the Soviet Union.

Yes, I believe, as charged, that Somoza was relatively mild compared to the Sandinistas. He was an autocrat, not a totalitarian, as was the Russian Czar, also mild compared to the Communists. Exile to Siberia under the Czar did not mean being worked to death, as testified to by Lenin himself in his memoirs. It does now. And only a few thousand were sent—not the vast Gulag population the Soviets created. Under Somoza there were acts of tyranny, corruption, and cruelty (as there are now), but also an opposition, an opposition press, freedom, private business, and an unfettered church. Somoza stole. But the country was more prosperous than it is now.

Professor Farer writes, "The Sandinista government will create conditions conducive to its reformation...isolation and external threats delay the day...if the Sandinistas are left free to achieve their objectives in the fields of education and health they will ultimately produce demands for true democratization."

The trouble is not with "demands for true democratization." It is with the Sandinistas' unwillingness to fulfill them. Their "objectives in the fields of education," like Cuba's and the Soviet Union's, are thoroughgoing indoctrination, not learning. I do not know about demands for democratization in Cuba and the Soviet Union. But despite education and "demands," I see little hope for

Castro's regime, or that of the Soviets, to become democratic. Professor Farer's belief that, somehow, the Sandinistas will give in to the democratic wishes of their subjects is a fantasy that flies in the face of all our experience. Experience shows, as I noted before, that rightist dictatorships sometimes can be peacefully transformed into democracies. There is not a single case on record where this has happened with a dictatorial leftist regime such as that of the Sandinistas. I'm all for education, but to believe that it produces democracy is a *non sequitur*; Hitler showed as much. The Germans were all too well educated. Education does not even produce much common sense, as shown by Professor Farer's belief in Sandinista democratization. He is a very educated man. But education has not affected his willful naïveté.

Professor Farer feels that the Sandinistas are more likely to secure human rights in the future than the government of El Salvador or Honduras. Well, the future is all unknown. I wouldn't bet on the Sandinistas, and I know too little about Honduras or El Salvador to bet. But certainly these two countries, despite guerillas, have more freedom than Nicaragua. Here Professor Farer tells us he does not want to refer to democracy because people who voted for Reagan "insist on equating democracy with elections in which parties compete, the electorate is protected from overt intimidation, and its ballots are counted accurately." I do "insist." Indeed, Farer stumbled on a pretty good definition of democracy as a political system. I am willing to endorse it. (You cannot have the things he lists without freedom of speech and assembly.) I hope Farer will endorse his own definition of democracy, attributed to Reaganites, and join me in opposing governments that deny people the right to choose among competing parties without intimidation.

Farer is right in saying that in many Latin American countries the democratically elected government has a tough time imposing its policies on military and other organized interests. Quite so. There is little we can do to help these democratic governments. But we should do it. One thing we certainly should not do is to support their replacement by leftist dictatorships. That would make matters much worse. Ultimately, the power of the military can be reduced and even eliminated, as Argentina, Brazil, and Uruguay have shown. Communists once in power can be removed only by war.

Professor Farer also suggests that "extreme economic inequality, mass illiteracy, ill health, and extreme economic insecurity...disable" a country from having a functioning democracy. I do not like poverty or illiteracy any better than he does. Yet they have not prevented democracy in India. In Nicaragua it is not poverty that prevents democracy, but the Sandinistas. It is not poverty, or illiteracy, that prevents democracy in Cuba either. Nor does literacy create it, as Castro shows and Hitler did before him. I'd rather have democracy, even if there is illiteracy, then literacy with Castro or Stalin. Democracy and literacy are both desirable. But neither depends on the other, as India shows, nor does one produce the other, as Hitler, Castro, and Stalin have shown.

IV

CHAPTER 7

# Nicaragua in Regional Context
## Aligning Ends and Means

### TOM J. FARER

Three propositions form the core of Professor van den Haag's defense of Reagan administration policy toward Nicaragua. One is that the Sandinista regime is unalterably hostile to the United States and reflexively supportive of the Soviet Union. Another is that these facts constitute a national security problem of sufficient weight to justify a modest investment for the purpose of mitigating or liquidating it. The third is that, for a country as wealthy as the United States, the cost of bleeding the Sandinistas by supporting the Contras is trivial—one hundred million or so dollars per annum out of a gross national product in excess of three trillion dollars. Even on the most pessimistic assumptions about Contra capabilities, he believes that cost should be borne. Although they may never overcome, at a minimum the Contras preoccupy the comandantes and drain Nicaraguan resources that would otherwise be available either to aid extant insurgencies elsewhere in central America or to develop Nicaragua into a more solid platform for future efforts to export revolution.

It is not quite clear to me just what Professor van den Haag feels about the costs to the Nicaraguan people. Thousands dead and crippled; tens of thousands bereaved; poverty prolonged, even intensified, for the great majority. In the humanitarian system of accounts, these costs are not trivial. But to a true believer in *realpolitik*, they are irrelevant, unless they somehow weaken the United States as a player in the game of nations. The general view of interstate relations that appears to inform Professor van den Haag's arguments tends to identify him as a believer.

Be that as it may, he seems to have anticipated this sort of sentimental concern by imputing grave violations of human rights to the Nicaraguan government and, if I understand him correctly, implying that these violations stem principally from the character of the regime rather than the passions and felt necessities of conducting a civil war. In other words, he appears to believe that the Nicaraguan people would suffer no less if the United States had never exerted itself to organize, arm, and train the Contra armies and did not currently provide logistical support for their belligerent and terroristic activities inside Nicaragua. It is, I hope, clear that I find this claim unpersuasive. The Sandinistas are not paragons, but unlike the military masters of El Salvador and Guatemala, they have not yet employed mass murder as an instrument of governance. They are not democrats forced into an authoritarian posture by the imperatives of self-defense. But, for the reasons I have sketched, evolution of a more pluralist political order in Nicaragua—particularly if the United States and its allies employed to that end the carrot-and-stick economic and political strategy I have also sketched—is no less likely than the outbreak of authentic pluralism in Honduras, El Salvador, Guatemala, and other countries where the Reagan administration purports to be building pluralism by means of sympathetic and constructive engagement.

Whether or not Professor van den Haag accepts my view that the humanitarian implications of current U.S. policy are important in themselves, he should share my concern for their impact in the realm of grand strategy. He should, but what I cannot tell is whether he does. In part because many politically active Americans associate one or another degree of moral squalor with current policy in Central America, it cannot attract broad political support. As Contragate has now revealed, executive branch determination to proceed without such support slides smoothly into subversion of Constitutional restraints. Thus, the pursuit of a minor strategic interest, albeit a presidential obsession, generates costs to the national interest of a far higher order than an annual hundred-million-dollar dollop of aid. Other than the protection of our sovereignty and territorial integrity, there is no more important national interest than the preservation of those limits on executive power that are a defining feature of a democratic political order.

The moral issue also insinuates itself into grand strategy through its impact outside the United States, particularly among the educated and among leaders of the popular classes in the Caribbean Basin. Support for the Contras tends to reinforce a widely held image of the United States as the enemy of social and political reform and hence of the humanitarian values reform is deemed to serve. This image is, of course, not uniformly unpopular. On the contrary, many military officers and most oligarchs celebrate it. So if their active cooperation with the United States or simply their local dominance guaranteed the advancement of our enduring interests in the Western Hemisphere, and if they seemed likely to retain or, where it is lost, to reclaim power at little cost to the United States, a reputation for hostility to reform would seem at worst harmless. Reality does not happen to coincide with either condition.

The nation's image in Latin America and expectations it necessarily induces about U.S. policy influenced the postrevolutionary dialectic of U.S.–Nicaraguan relations. Spiraling mutual suspicion shading into hostility was an almost inevitable consequence of the Sandinistas' conviction that the United States would sooner or later move against any program of egalitarian social reform. The Sandinistas behaved as if certain that conflict was inevitable. If it did not make conflict inevitable, their certainty made it likely irrespective of all other conditions.

El Salvador demonstrates that averting revolutions can be no less costly than efforts to reverse them. Quite apart from its extraordinary drain on the time, energy, and imagination of senior political, military, and diplomatic personnel, El Salvador has claimed over a billion dollars in American economic and military aid since 1979. The prospect is for more of the same. Although aid is defended in part on the grounds of its supposed capacity to facilitate the political and social reforms most American experts regard as necessary for the restoration of civic peace, I will explain below how, in practice, the aid liquidates incentives for, and empowers military and civilian enemies of, those reforms.

That Washington's attempt to maintain or, in the case of Nicaragua, restore, traditional structures of political, economic, and social power in the Caribbean Basin is costly seems indisputable. Less apparent, however, is the doubtful consistency of that tactical objective with our overall interests in the area. In order to understand how we may be buying means that are not only costly but incongruent with our ends, it is necessary first to clarify those ends and then to examine the influence of U.S. policy on the internal dynamics of the region's principal nonrevolutionary states.

## Ends

A conventional yet candid statement of American ends would assume something like the following form: What we seek above all are governments willing to cooperate with the United States in handling the wide range of issues that this country cannot deal with satisfactorily through unilateral action. These issues include regional security, economic relations (political acts and omissions that stimulate or inhibit the movement of goods, services, and capital), drugs, and immigration. Conservative governments, whether democratic or authoritarian, are generally cooperative because their interests coincide broadly with ours, above all in the security field. Conversely, governments of the left are by their nature uncooperative. Worse than that, they create new problems to burden the agenda of the United States and its allies. Hence, the preservation of conservative governments and the replacement of those with revolutionary objectives is an intermediate goal of high importance.

Although most members of the American foreign policy community would, I fear, regard that statement as a collection of self-evident truths, every one of its propositions is in fact problematical. It is, to begin with, evident that cooperativeness (which in practice tends to mean agreement with Washington's definition of the problem and Washington's solution) is itself only a means for achieving substantive ends. A government, although cooperative to the point of servility, may lack the strength or competence to implement policies that foster American objectives. And a government inclined by ideology to doubt the coincidence of its interests with those of the United States may *incidentally* promote our ends through the effective implementation of domestic policies adopted in a spirit of total indifference to their impact on other states. Until we look more closely at the substance of enduring U.S. interests and at the complex obstacles to their full realization, we cannot adequately assess the instrumental value of ideological affinity and military dependence and their corollary of cooperativeness. Nor can we persuasively conclude that conservative governments are worth the cost of perpetuating them.

Analysts of national interest invariably begin with security issues. In regard to them, what should we want from our neighbors? The answer is that for the defense of the hemisphere *from external attack*, we require neither armed forces to supplement our own nor bases. The military establishment we maintain principally to support our goals in other parts of the world coincidentally provides the means requisite for defending the hemisphere under any plausible scenario of external assault, assuming there is one. Force supplements and bases are useful (though hardly essential) only on the assumption that the interests of the United States require a capability for intervening in Western Hemisphere states to determine the outcome of civil wars or, as Washington conventionally prefers to put it, to "combat subversion."

To justify blank-check support of conservative governments

on the grounds that we require their cooperation in order to maintain conservative governments is to argue in a circle. Advocates of traditional United States policy for the Hemisphere must invoke other reasons. Common among them is the concern that leftist governments will facilitate the projection of Soviet military power by providing bases, intelligence, and proxies. On this point, as I suggested earlier, arguments also tend toward circularity. If, out of conviction about their inevitable collaboration with Soviet power, the United States reflexively seeks to destroy leftist governments, for survival if for no other reason the latter will reflexively attempt to induce Soviet collaboration.

Being sensitive to this charge of circularity, American rightists have insisted on the sufficiency of an overpowering anti-American animus to explain the Soviet Union's relationship with Cuba, as well as its much looser and more limited collaboration with Nicaragua. Any jury willing to take a dispassionate view of the evidence—including the variety of relationships leftist or even self-described Communist regimes in different parts of the globe have worked out with the Soviet Union—must return a verdict on this claim of "not proven."

All that can be said with confidence is that, as long as the United States acts to sustain its earned reputation as the enemy of revolutionary regimes (including that of Mexico during the 1920s and early 1930s), leftist governments will feel the need to solicit such support as they can get from the Soviet bloc. But after Nicaragua's experience, they will solicit with the expectation of a decidedly restrained response. That restraint suggests that the Soviet Union either sees little to be gained from strategic cooperation with a Caribbean Basin state other than Cuba (assuming it does not regret acquiring that $4 billion-a-year habit) or is convinced that wherever such cooperaiton might yield substantial benefits, it will not be tolerated by the United States. Whichever calculation controls Soviet behavior, it would appear that, without the cost of guaranteeing ideologically congenial regimes in neighboring states, the

United States can realize its security objective of averting a significantly increased Soviet military presence in the hemisphere.

I would like to put military issues aside for a moment and turn to other areas of concern to assess the fit of means and ends. Any list would have to include illegal immigration, debt, petroleum, and, possibly, markets. Plenary control over immigration is a defining feature of sovereignty. Like all independent countries, the United States has it in theory. But enormous pressure to enter this country, coming primarily from the Caribbean Basin, has made control in fact increasingly tenuous.

Since the two most visible immigrant tides to wash over American shores during the past 60 years came in the wake of third world revolutions, one of them Latin, the Right's imputation of a uniquely close relationship between revolution and massive emigration with ensuing pressure to enter the United States is as plausible as it is misleading. The Cuban and Vietnamese migrations captured public attention in part because they were compressed into narrow time lines, in part because they were catalyzed by dramatic external events, and in part because, for political and ideological reasons, the U.S. government formally opened the nation's door to them, so entry could be a public event. But the immigration problem that drove Congress to impose unprecedented obligations on employers and to take the extraordinary step of legitimating the permanent presence in the United States of persons who entered illegally and are believed to number in the millions had nothing to do with the emergence of revolutionary governments.

While these millions have come principally from Mexico, the Dominican Republic, Haiti, and other small, non-Communist states are also substantial contributors to the illegal stream. While political persecution may have driven a few of the Haitians, who have braved hardships and dangers nearly as grave as those faced by southeast Asia's Boat People, the primary catalysts of their migration have been fearful poverty in Haiti—not unrelated to the vicious kleptocracy under which they endure—and the known proximity and affluence of the United States. Anyone familiar with Haiti knows that if the United States would give Haitians the same exceptional access tendered to refugees from Communist countries, the country's tiny elite would be left with no one to govern.

Revolutons are not the only political events that generate refugees. The right-wing military *coup d'état* in Chile drove close to a half million people out of that country. Mexico has provided refuge for tens of thousands of Guatemalan Indians driven from their homes by the government's merciless repression. Even democratic governments may act so as to feed the refugee stream; Palestinian Arabs discoverd this after the 1967 Middle East War. Revolutions are, moreover, Johnny-come-latelies as emigration generators. Long before Karl Marx was a gleam in his mother's eye, conservative monarchs forced the mass migration of Jews and Moslems from Spain and Arcadians from Nova Scotia. And it was conservative governments of every sort that rounded up millions of black men, women, and children and sent them in chains on a migration no less heartless than the ones organized in our century by Hitler and Stalin.

As is true of so many social phenomena, while political events are the dramatic causes, economics, exerting its relentless pressure, is the most important one. In only a few cases did direct political pressure impel the vast host of European migrants who, from the 17th to the 20th centuries, surged successively into the Western Hemisphere. They came for the same reason that during the present era drew two million Colombians into Venezuela, several millions of Africans from neighboring states into Nigeria and South Africa, respectively, and many more millions of southern Europeans and North Africans into France, Germany, Switzerland, the Low Countries, and Scandinavia. They came to escape the most enduring of all villains—Poverty.

Even if the United States and its various indigenous allies succeeded in liquidating every revolutionary movement and government in the Caribbean Basin, hopeless poverty would continue herding people toward our frontiers. Sustained rates of economic growth well in excess of population growth will help only at the margin, because so little of any increment in national wealth trickles down to the lower classes. They cannot participate as farmers in processes of growth. Throughout the greater part of Latin America, land is distributed with a degree of inequality unmatched in other parts of the third world. And even those who have managed to retain decent-size plots may only scratch a living, because credit and irrigation and other public or semipublic goods are channeled to the rich.

Only a relative few participate as workers. This is so in part because the upper classes have used their political power to manipulate exchange rates and tariffs so as to reduce the real cost of imported, labor-saving technology. But the principal reason is that the paucity of land, coupled with the mitigation of communicable diseases (which, after all, cannot be securely quarantined among the poor), has created a reserve army of the unemployed to serve as a perpetual drag on wages.

If these states could match the growth rates of the highest achievers—South Korea, Taiwan, and (particularly in the late 1960s and early 1970s) Brazil—some ensuing shrinkage in the reserve army would at least generate a little hope. But those states "took off" in an era when the markets of developed states were peculiarly receptive to penetration by third-world-processed and -manufactured goods and oil prices were very low. In addition, their internal conditions were far more favorable to growth.

The southeast Asian prodigies had completed land reforms on a scale justifying the name of revolution, albeit arranged at the top by conservative and authoritarian governments and culminating not in massive collectives and cooperatives but in family farms. Practicing a labor-intensive agriculture, their owners developed quickly into a rural bourgeoisie that provided ballast for the political system and a relatively broad domestic market for light industrial goods. Reform fostered investment and assured widespread participation in its fruits. Among all the capitalist developing states of Asia, the Middle East, and Latin America, South Korea and Taiwan appear to be the only ones where rapid growth did not intensify inequality. They are also unique in their ability to match rapid growth in national product with unusually rapid improvement in overall levels of social welfare as measured by longevity and infant mortality rates.

Brazil, with one-third of Latin America's population, could offer its own and foreign investors the attraction of a large domestic market, even after discounting for the 30% who were destitute and the additional 30% or so who were merely poor. But because it did not take off from ground prepared by political and social reform, growth aggravated inequality and, according to some economists, diminished in absolute terms the living standards of the lowest 40%. The concentration of poverty in the northeast and the swell of affluence from São Paulo south triggered a massive migration out of the poverty zone.

Mexico is another Latin state available to demonstrate how, under contemporary conditions, a high growth rate, sustained over three decades and neither preceded nor accompanied by social and political reform, can bypass a huge slice of the national population. Having its own pole of affluence and being far from any other, Brazil experienced only internal migration. Were it as close as Mexico to the United States, Portuguese might well be the principal tongue among America's undocumented aliens.

Distinctive inequality of wealth, income, power, status, and opportunity—inherited in most cases from the colonial era and reinforced in all by both state and market power—is the norm for most non-English-speaking Caribbean Basin states. We may therefore conclude, on the basis of evidence accumulating over the past 40 years, that, in the absence of major social and political reforms, most of these countries will continue to generate intense pressure for the export of population. Therefore, unless the United States militarizes its frontiers, it will continue to experience large-scale illegal immigration.

This is the prospect even assuming growth rather than contraction in the economies of traditional exporters, and even assuming those that currently have relatively inclusive and hence legitimized political systems and relatively effective governments will continue to have them. Remove those assumptions and the prospective tide of illegal immigration becomes a tidal wave. Remove those linked assumptions, and other United States objectives—assured access to oil, an orderly structure for handling Latin debt, expanding markets for United States exports—pass over the horizon.

Whatever one may conclude concerning the appropriateness of alternative means for servicing our *military* interests in the arc embracing the Caribbean, Central America, and the northern edge of South America, with respect to other interests, the test of any proposed means is: Will it further political and social reform in all countries and the maintenance of relatively inclusive political systems and effective governments, particularly in those countries that are large debtors, currently or potentially significant trading partners, and/or providers of oil? The Reagan administration's effort to destroy the leftist insurgency in El Salvador and the leftist government in Nicaragua does not pass that test.

As I noted in Part I, the Contadora states have political systems that are relatively open, inclusive, and, with the arguable exception of little Panama, stable. The comparison I had in mind when I used the word *relatively* was with a large group of Latin American capitalist states including El Salvador, Guatemala, Honduras, Bolivia, Chile, and Paraguay. If the comparison were to be made solely in terms of stability, one could add Argentina, Ecuador, and Peru to the list, although each is now struggling to consolidate a competitive politics.

While being stable in comparison to many Latin American states, the Contadora political systems are nevertheless brittle when compared to those of capitalist democracies in North America and Western Europe. They are brittle for reasons whose explanatory value varies considerably among the four. One is that they lack the resources needed to provide a population-wide floor under destitution; their inability to offer at least the prospect of relief from extreme poverty is delegitimizing. A second, closely related, is the conspicuous inequality that marks them all. It makes it possible to see lower-class misery as the result not of an absolute insufficiency of national wealth but rather of the system of political economy that distributes it.

A third reason is the absence of Horatio Alger myths and a supporting structure of entrepreneurial opportunity to ease the frustration of middle-class youth. (The drug trade in Colombia seems to be the most notable exception to this generalization.) A fourth, least applicable to Venezuela, is the evident centralization of political power in a small elite and the consequent discrepancy between the democratic ideals celebrated by governing elites and the reality over which they preside. People who feel, and in fact are, excluded from the exercise of power, who are objects rather than subjects of the system, cannot feel a passionate proprietary attachment to it. The gap between ideal and reality has the capacity to transform passive alienation into active grievance. A fifth is deterioration in their economic performance after the good years of the 1960s and 1970s, a factor of particular importance for Mexico and Venezuela. And a sixth, endemic to all of Latin America, is a tendency toward ideological polarization, with the Right perpetually dubious about popular participation in governance and disinclined to regard the institutions and parties of the Left as legitimate players in the political game. Left and Right tend to see each other as mortal enemies with incompatible objectives.

With all that centrifugal potential, why does the center hold? Certainly one facet of the explanation is that government is not experienced by most of the population primarily as a parasite. The public sector employs substantial numbers of people and delivers goods and services to many more. By demonstrating through the allocation of goods and services that loyalty to the system pays dividends, its managers reinforce the structure of power.

A second source of stability for the reigning political systems is their relative inclusiveness. The elite who run them treat spokesmen and institutions of the lower and middle classes as legitimate participants in the political game, as long, of course, as they accept its rules. Inclusion means that their claims must be taken into account and that they must have some opportunity to compete for some measure of power.

Relative freedom of expression and association—a function of elite confidence and ideology—encourage open, nonviolent dissidence and provide a political safety valve. Together with other signs of adherence to basic human rights norms—above all in official repudiation of arbitrary arrest, torture, and summary execution as tactics for maintaining public order—they operate to strengthen the political order's legitimacy.

Size and complexity also buttress stability in the principal Contadora states by discouraging political organization around a single issue threatening to the established order. In countries like El Salvador and Guatemala, land reform is reasonably seen as an instrument for transforming the entire system. It is doubtful that any single substantive reform could have such tremendous consequences in Colombia, Mexico, and Venezuela. Moreover, the size and complexity of their social and economic systems create conflicts of interest *within* the middle and lower classes that obstruct formation of a system-challenging coalition.

But no factor seems more important to the survival of centrist rule than the broadly shared perception of an authentic and dignified national existence: of a distinctive history and culture and of space for the exercise of political autonomy. The United States contributes to stability when it demonstrates respect for the views of Contadora governments and, conversely, contributes to instability when it humiliates them either by dismissing their diplomacy or demanding that it conform to a definition of shared self-interest made in Washington, D.C.

As it has acted out its obsession with military victories in Central America, the administration of Ronald Reagan has belittled, when it could not ignore, Contadora diplomacy. If it has not actually attempted to coerce or suborn any Contadora state, it has at a minimum allowed the dissemination of rumors to that effect. Thus, it has already behaved in ways tending to erode political order in Colombia, Mexico, and Venezuela. If the administration follows its instincts and makes war against Nicaragua by dispatching troops or air cover, it will put a great deal of additional strain on the political systems of these natural friends of the United States and, in all likelihood, force a diplomatic confrontation with one or more of them, as well as most of the other major Latin members of the Organization of American States.

Instead of reviving American leadership in the hemisphere, Ronald Reagan will have done more than all his modern predecessors to inter it. Whatever their hidden desires, political leaders in states that are not satellites of the United States, nor ruled by dictators or soldiers, will find cooperation with Washington on other issues — for example, trade, debt, investment, migration, narcotics — gravely inhibited by popular hostility to U.S. intervention. Not even the most inflated claims about the strategic consequences of a consolidated Sandinista regime in Nicaragua come close to offsetting the predictable impact of intervention on the Contadora states and on inter-American diplomatic relations, not to mention its disintegrative effect on the American polity.

## Central America

Not only are the purposes and tactics of this administration costly in any rational accounting of the national interest, they are also in certain respects contradictory. In order fully to appreciate the contradictory features of administration policy, it is helpful to look at Nicaragua's Central American neighbors.

*Costa Rica.* It is in but not of Central America, a broad-based and solidly established political democracy whose two dominant political parties, like their Venezuelan counterparts, hold the agenda and discourse of politics near the ideological center. Democracy with all the trappings (free speech, press, and association, a relatively independent and impartial judiciary, due process) is one of the country's five defining features, arguably the cumulative expression of the other four: a level of concentration in land ownership below the Latin American norm (albeit one that has grown worse over the past two decades), the absence of a regular army with its inevitable concomitant of an institutionalized officer corps, a welfare state unusual in its breadth and depth for a country at Costa Rica's stage of economic growth, and a comparatively homogeneous, primarily European, population. Since Argentina, with a similar population mix, is only now showing signs of developing effective democratic institutions and a matching culture, I am inclined to discount, albeit not to exclude, that factor as an explanation of Costa Rica's achievements.

While the pattern of land distribution results in large measure from adventitious circumstances of colonial occupation and rule, the phenomenon of the demilitarized state is a modern product. In 1948 the country's political elite took up the gun to resolve an internal electoral dispute. The faction led by Pepe Figueres, an aggressive young planter, won the fight and then disbanded the regular army. Don Pepe and his colleagues recognized that while they lived under the shadow of the United States, they lived as well under its protection from external attack. They recognized, in other words, that the only real function for a regular army in Central America has been to foster social mobility for middle-class lads with a taste for violence and loot and to repress challenges to the distribution of wealth and power. Believing that the distribution of income and wealth in Costa Rica was not widely felt to be unjust, and determined to construct a welfare state that would, among other things, marshal a large part of the population behind the institutions of liberal democracy, Figueres regarded an officer corps as a cluster of vices without compensating virtues.

Since 1949, the Costa Rican constitution has prohibited formation of a regular army. Maintenance of public order has been the responsibility of a lightly armed civil and rural guard operating under the direction of political appointees and absorbing a very small fraction of national wealth. Both as an indirect consequence of the U.S. effort to overthrow the government of Nicaragua and as a result of direct pressure from Washington, Costa Ricans can see the first signs of the remilitarization of society.

By covertly fostering a Costa Rican front for guerrilla operations against Nicaragua, the Reagan administration has created pressure within Costa Rica to upgrade the capabilities of the rural guard so that it can more effectively control border areas. Moreover, as a consequence of Nicaraguan antiguerrilla operations along the border and reports of Nicaraguan cross-border operations against guerrilla camps, the Costa Rican government has been pushed toward a more general enhancement of the military instrument. Signs of direct pressure to that end include a 1981 statement by Jeane Kirkpatrick, U.S. Ambassador to the U.N., that Costa Rica might need U.S. military assistance (leading President Rodrigo Carazo to demand letters of apology for interference in Costa Rica's internal affairs) and proposals from Washington that Costa Rica participate in U.S.-organized war games, send observers to meetings of the Central American Defense Council (CONDECA, a U.S.-sponsored mechanism to facilitate military cooperation primarily among the armed forces of El Salvador, Guatemala, and Honduras), and send guardsmen for training in Honduras.

The pattern of Costa Rica's response to direct and indirect pressure for remilitarization has been one of resistance followed by at least partial relinquishment of its initial position. For instance, in the very year President Carazo denounced the suggestion that his government might require military assistance, he agreed to the renewal of the U.S. security assistance program that had lapsed 13 years earlier. And despite his successor's initial rejection of the Reagan administration's offer to train guardsmen in programs based outside Costa Rica, by 1983 the U.S. Army had begun training civil guards in Panama and Fort Benning, Georgia. In 1985 a contingent of Green Berets arrived in Costa Rica itself to conduct additional training programs. These training activities were part of the government's effort to expand the country's internal security forces. In addition to increasing the size and capability of the guards, President Monge, who assumed office in 1982, established and began arming a civilian militia that by 1985 had about ten thousand members. Its uses thus far have included breaking a hospital workers' strike.

That particular use symbolizes three things: the marginal role of working-class organizations in the country's politics; the extent to which the costs of the austerity the country is experiencing in the 1980s, after two decades of solid growth, are borne by the lower classes; and the incipient polarization of political life with concomitant recourse to violence by fanatics of the Left and the Right. Although there have only been a few incidents so far, both because they are virtually unprecedented in postwar Costa Rica and because of the feverish environment in which they occur, they are ominous.

Even if the United States were attempting to insulate Costa Rican democracy from the Nicaraguan war, the war would be adding strain to a political system already burdened by grave economic problems. Between 1981 and 1986, per capita gross domestic product declined by 11%. The precipitous fall in the price of bananas and coffee exposed the costs of an inflated and poorly managed public sector that employs close to 20% of the entire work force.

Independent of its direct and planned impact on the region's one authentic democracy, U.S. strategy for and operations in Central America seriously inhibit Costa Rican efforts to diversify exports, to shrink and reshape the public sector, and to devise economic and social policies better able to reconcile growth with middle-class expectations and with lower-class demands for a minimally decent existence. If our principal goal were a Central America populated by stable democracies, we would be going about it in an ass-backwards way.

*El Salvador.* Before the coup of 1979 that overturned the regime of General Carlos Humberto Romero, no one even passingly familiar with this country would have disputed the proposition that it possessed every ugly feature so arrestingly absent in Costa Rica: brutal and parasitic armed forces; prodigious concentration of land ownership and, for that matter, all other forms of wealth and status (epitomized by the conventional reference to El Salvador as the land of the Fourteen Families); political institutions that hid the substance of tyranny behind the thin, mocking forms of constitutional democracy.

El Salvador exemplified the not uncommon longevity of harsh authoritarian rule. Independence from Spain, achieved in the early 19th century, had not fundamentally altered the political and social order established during the colonial era. It had simply meant that the handful of great landowning families could rule undisturbed by Spanish bureaucrats and had to use a homegrown army rather than Spanish troops as their instrument for repressing and disciplining the peasant, largely Indian, masses.

Among the several great pools of destitution in the world—sub-Saharan Africa, South Asia, Latin America—the latter is distinguished by the degree to which the ownership of land is concentrated in so few hands. But even in an area where concentration is the norm, El Salvador was in this respect notorious.

The coup of 1979 was the fifth reformist bid for power since the mid-1940s. The ruling coalition of officers content with the pickings of the *status quo* and economic royalists had quickly liquidated the earlier attempts. In 1979 the reformers were again a distinct minority of the officers' corps. They were, moreover, primarily of junior rank. Yet for a moment it appeared that, in collaboration with political figures of the democratic left, they would drag both the military institution and Salvadoran society as a whole across the threshold of a new order. This seemed possible because they had working for them a force that in the Salvadoran jungle is far more potent than moral authority or simple justice. They had fear.

Mass unrest twisted through city streets and country lanes. Aided by students and priests, the workers and peasants and certain lower-middle-class groups, particularly teachers, had achieved an unparalleled degree of mobilization in the form of "popular organizations" conducting strikes and demonstrations and by their very existence threatening the sort of mass uprising with a trained guerrilla vanguard that had only months earlier forced the collapse of the Somoza regime. The Nicaraguan revolution itself undermined confidence among officers in government by slaughter. No less demoralizing than the triumph of revolutionary forces was the refusal of an American president to veto it.

Purporting to speak in the name of the armed forces, the coup makers declared in favor of free elections, free speech, freedom of action for political parties and labor organizations, a more equitable distribution of land, and an end to corruption and violence. Among the obstacles to translating these arresting goals into public policy was the character of the military institution—its tradition of absolute independence from civilian control, its tradition of respect for the hierarchy of rank, its symbiotic affinity with the oligarchs, its opportunities for social mobility and loot. A second, as it turned out, was the intransigence of the armed Left; initially the guerrillas treated the coup not as a fleeting opportunity to come in from the cold and build a viable reform coalition but as a breach in the old order through which they could race to total victory. The third was the reaction of the Carter administration, already in transit back to a more conventional, bipolar view of the world, partially because of Soviet adventures outside the Western Hemisphere and partially in response to incipient difficulties with the Sandinistas. While the administration welcomed the coup's promise of democratic reform, it was determined not to watch a replay of the Nicaraguan rising culminating with the nondemocratic Left in absolute control. It did not, therefore, urge the military reformers to pursue negotiations with the guerrillas, or even with the leaders of the popular organizations, since they were seen as collaborators at best, if not simply as a lightly veiled, above-ground extension of the guerrillas. In short, the White House committed itself to building a reform coalition strictly out of military dissidents and Center to Center–Left politicians. But it equally committed itself to the survival of the Salvadoran armed forces.

The initial reaction of those forces suggested that some officers recognized this dual commitment and construed it as a license to butcher the guerrillas and anyone suspected of aiding them, intentionally or otherwise, while carrying out economic reforms, particularly those calculated to sop up popular discontent at the fastest possible pace. Others either concluded that the United States was back in the business of guaranteeing the survival of regimes threatened by the Left or decided that, whatever Washington's preferences, slaughter unleavened by reform would suffice. The latter collaborated with the former on the slaughter side of things while at the same time working, in conjunction with the oligarchs, to isolate military reformers of every stripe. The unofficial death squads that some sectors of the upper class began to underwrite, after recovering from the initial shock of the coup, were filled with military moonlighters as well as social dregs.

When the civilian adherents of the original junta found themselves unable to halt the massacre, and found as well that they themselves or political associates were targeted by some of its perpetrators, they withdrew. Their departure left the Christian Democrats as the only credible civilian group willing to link arms with the armed forces. Together they formed a second junta. As the killing spiraled upward, the junta announced a sweeping land reform and nationalization of banks and export companies. Control of land, credit, and the process of exportation had been the three pillars of oligarchic rule. Hence, the reform appeared to mark a truly radical break with the past. But many of those civilians who had struggled for years to make reform possible could not stomach the wave of murder that accompanied it, particularly after it reached distinguished members of their own Christian Democrat party, including the attorney general, Mario Zamora. Their consequent withdrawal from the junta and the government pretty much reduced the civilian facade of military rule to a single man, Napoleon Duarte.

Nothing he subsequently does can quite erase the fact that Duarte remained in the junta while the death squads roamed at will, leaving a trail of corpses. Not only did he remain—and his presence alone eased President Reagan's task of extracting arms from a Congress less inclined than he to finance mass murder; in addition he was mute. And when he was not mute, he was an apologist. As the distinguished journalist Christopher Dickey reported in June 1983, Duarte continually delivered anesthetic messages to the foreign press, assuring it that, as a consequence of Christian Democrat participation in the government, a "process of control" over the armed forces was occurring. While he wove visions of civilian rule, the stench of death rose higher.

Being wrong then about the "process" does not guarantee that he is wrong now. Is there at least a credible scenario for establishing civilian control of the military and for satisfying the other conditions necessary for an enduring peace? The one sketched by Duarte during his 1984 presidential campaign looked roughly as follows: By virtue of his electoral mandate, his consequent moral authority, his noble ideals, and his ability to secure economic and military aid, he would succeed in subordinating the military institution to civilian authority. Subordination would produce a climate of security for all those willing to play politics by democratic rules.

Coincidentally, he would complete the process of economic and social reform. Since it was despair over ever achieving reform by means of electoral politics that had populated the ranks of the violent Left, neither its social democratic partners nor its mass base among workers, peasants, and students would have any further reason for collaboration. Thus isolated, the comandantes would either have to accept amnesty and peaceful political struggle or face liquidation.

It is a pretty vision. But it is not a very plausible one, to begin with because insofar as establishing control over the military insti-

tution is concerned, Duarte seems in most respects to occupy a
weaker position today than at the beginning of the decade, when he
failed. The reformers have been purged. And fear has diminished:
in part because the death squads decimated the Left's urban infrastructure and the popular organizations; in part because over a half
billion dollars in military aid has funded the tripling of the armed
forces and their equipment with sophisticated modern arms; in
larger measure because the Reagan administration has given them a
flat commitment manifested in words (that call El Salvador a supreme test of national will to resist Communist expansion) and
deeds (resisting congressional efforts to write human rights conditions into aid legislation, and certifying compliance—in cynical disregard of the facts—with whatever conditions have episodically
been imposed).

If a stable and democratic country is Washington's goal, one
can say that it has created a perverse set of incentives. In the name
of victory over the Left, the Reagan administration has opened the
treasury of the United States to the congenitally corrupt Salvadoran
officer corps. It now enjoys undreamed-of access to money—
money subject to appropriation by means both legitimate and ille-
gitimate—assuming the distinction exists for the military institution. There is, by the way, no evidence that Duarte exercises
control over the level or allocation of military assistance. While the
country's civilian economy is in a state of acute depression, its
military economy experiences an unprecedented boom that seems
destined to continue as long as guerrillas remain a substantial force.
Hence, if they were left entirely alone, the officers might prefer
nothing more than the indefinite prolongation of the *status quo*. But
if, under the prodding of their growing cadre of U.S. advisors and
with their constantly growing firepower and mobility, they succeed
in destroying effective opposition, is it likely that they will then
accept that enormous contraction in their size and resources justified by the loss of a credible internal threat? Surely they will do
everything possible to maintain levels of funding. Since the U.S.

Congress will not, under those circumstances, continue its funding, the triumphant military institution will have powerful incentives to attach itself to the Salvador exchequer like an enormous leach. In neither event does one see the way clear either to real civilian government or to a revived and reformed civil society.

The central element in the second junta's program for social transformation, land reform, has been very partially realized, so partially that one might as accurately say that it has been largely frustrated. Implementation of its so-called phase II, distribution of the rich coffee plantations, was blocked by the parties of the Right, never enjoyed Reagan administration support, and now seems a dead letter. The Right also managed first to limit and then to roll back most of phase III, land to the tillers. The success of phase I—transformation of the largest but not wealthiest estates into cooperatives—remains highly problematical. Some peasant occupiers have been murdered or driven from the land. Others must pay protection money to local commanders. If the public sector does not provide surviving occupiers with adequate credit and other forms of support, they may ultimately go under.

The Reagan administration has not been merely indifferent to reform. On the contrary, consistent with its ideology and its desire to assure the Right's support for what at least has some of the look of a civilian government, it has pressured Duarte to placate the oligarchs and their retainers by reducing the public sector's role in the economy and, among other things, permitting the reestablishment of private banks. Privatization can be a prudent step in countries with many sophisticated participants in large and diverse markets. In El Salvador, where a handful of economic corsairs have traditionally monopolized commerce and finance, it is a recipe for restoration of the old order. Or whatever is left to restore.

I have spoken of the armed forces as implausible participants in the effort to build a reasonably stable, democratic, and just society. Reliance on the private sector to that end is still more anomalous. The orientation of its dominant figures is nicely summarized by a leading U.S. academic authority on El Salvador, Enrique Baloyra. What is at stake for the leaders of the private sector, he has written: "is not merely...whether the government should not bend too much in the direction of union demands spend too much on welfare, link public policy making to the electoral process, or try to push taxes beyond reasonable limits. The leaders of the reactionary coalition of El Salvador *do not believe in unions or in welfare or in suffrage."*

With such allies, the United States really does not need enemies. It is, therefore, not surprising that the policy encouraged and funded by the United States has produced the following results. Outside the cantonments of the armed forces, the condition of the country is desperate. Nearly 10% of the entire population is estimated to be in the United States as illegal immigrants. An additional several hundred thousand are internal refugees, in most cases driven off their land by the armed forces, who treat whole sections of the country as free fire zones. Additional thousands are refugees in Honduras and Costa Rica. Since 1981 the per capita national product has fallen by almost 20%. Roughly 40% of the potential work force is unemployed. Only U.S. economic assistance permits the economy to function at all. There is no foreign investment and little or no sign of local investment.

In the realm of institutional development the results are as bleak. Respect for human rights does not exist. The armed forces make little effort to distinguish between civilians and guerrillas in areas where the latter are active. Persons allegedly suspected of collaboration are detained solely at the will of the armed forces, held for open-ended periods without formal charge or hearing, and frequently tortured. Death squads continue to terrorize the population, although now they achieve their goal by means of carefully targeted executions. The rule of law does not exist. Well-connected persons are immune from legal process. Corruption and intimidation are the principal forms of legal argument.

*Enrique Baloyra, "The Model of Reactionary Despotism in Central America," in Martin Diskin, ed., *Trouble in our Backyard*, Pantheon, New York, 1983, p. 112.

All that is true because the elected government of Napoleon Duarte reigns without ruling. It exists, in other words, at the sufferance of the armed forces. Duarte has been entirely unsuccessful in subjecting them to legal process. For instance, a colonel implicated in a ring of kidnappers preying on wealthy Salvadorans simply refused to be prosecuted. When key commanders backed him, the effort was dropped. The officer corps continues to live by the motto of colonial officials and soldiers who received unappealing instructions from Madrid: *Obedezco, pero no cumplo* ("I obey, but I do not comply"). One of the few meetings with the opposition consented to by Duarte was aborted when the colonel responsible for security in the region ignored Duarte's orders to keep troops away from the town where the meeting was to be held.

Duarte won election on a platform promising peace and social reform. Neither can be achieved in the foreseeable future other than through a negotiated settlement with that part of the opposition willing to become one element in a larger coalition for reform. Calls for negotiations from the guerrillas and particularly from the exiled politicians of the old democratic Left are now ignored. The Reagan administration, the private sector, and the armed forces oppose concessions to the Left and vary in their attitude toward reform from indifference to feverish hostility. If stable democracy is our goal, we are on the wrong track.

*Guatemala.* This country is the Uganda of Latin America, a blood-soaked place of nightmarish cruelties, ruled by its unspeakable corps of officers—Murder, Incorporated, with a flag. Since 1954 successive generations of officers have waged campaigns of unrelenting brutality against critics of military rule and proponents of economic and social reform; against the armed and, more commonly, the unarmed; against advocates of violent revolution and advocates of gradual reform. They have made a graveyard, but they have not called it peace, preferring rather to treat the country as being in a permanent state of war, as a Hobbesian jungle where the military institution is the king of beasts. Jimmy Carter suspended their access to military aid but did nothing to shake their grip on Guatemala. Ronald Reagan has restored them to the status of honored ally.

The Salvadoran and Guatemalan military establishments have much in common: a deep sense of estrangement from civilian society, contempt for politicians and democratic rule, rejection of any criterion other than efficacy for evaluating their tactics, readiness to use military power for personal enrichment. There is, however, one happier parallel: From time to time both have been home to officers determined to address the awful inequities that pock their respective societies and to inspire civilians to take up the gun in a desperate effort to obtain the redress of grievances.

In Guatemala the reformers actually succeeded briefly in grasping power. In the early 1940s, they joined newly emergent middle-class forces in overthrowing the oligarchic dictator, Jorge Ubico, and inaugurating a decade of incipient social progress. Juan José Arévalo, the former schoolteacher who replaced Ubico, initiated reforms in land tenure and the conditions of rural labor. By the standards of most postwar land reform programs, he was extraordinarily solicitous of the great landowning interests. But for them— including the United Fruit Company, by far the largest owner—any public measure that trammeled their will was intolerable.

What was intolerable to United Fruit proved to be intolerable to the government of the United States. Its secretary of state in 1954, John Foster Dulles, had in private life been counsel to United Fruit. Together with his brother, Allen, director of the CIA, he organized a mixed force of Guatemalans and foreign mercenaries, applied diplomatic, economic, and psychological pressure, blocked a U.N. inquiry, manipulated the OAS, and succeeded in overthrowing Juan José Arévalo's elected successor, Jacobo Arbenz Guzmán, a former officer who had played a leading role in the revolution against the dictator Ubico. The counterrevolutionary government installed by the brothers Dulles purged the officers who had backed Arbenz, liquidated the hesitant but promising reforms of the prior decade, and set about reminding the incipient labor movement that Guatemala was no longer a free country, although it was once again a docile member in good standing of what the Dulles brothers, among others, liked to call the "free world."

The one virtually immutable source of contradiction in the armed forces of any nation, including a superpower client, is the generic association of military establishments with the protection of national sovereignty. While the gun gives them power, it is that mission, if anything, that gives them respect. Hence, a military establishment in the service of a foreign power is, in the Platonic sense, a contradiction in terms.

In terms of the ideal conception of the national armed forces, to exist solely as a guard for the rich is degrading enough. But where the *primus inter pares* of the rich is a foreign company, soldiers plumb new depths. For idealistic officers, it is a source of self-disgust. Only six years after the counterrevolution, what must have been simmering dissatisfaction among some military elements flamed into revolt when the armed forces leadership allowed the CIA to use Guatemalan soil as a staging base for the planned invasion of Cuba. With the help of air strikes flown by Cubans trained by the CIA for participation in the Bay of Pigs invasion, the revolt was finally crushed. Officers who survived were purged. Some of them, including two outstanding men trained in the United States for counterinsurgent operations, went into the hills and formed the first guerrilla movement.

With arms and training provided by the United States pursuant to the Alliance for Progress, the government responded with its first counterinsurgency campaign. Using the tactics that would soon become time-honored in Guatemala—indiscriminate slaughter—the guerrillas were gradually liquidated. But since the conditions from which they had germinated did not change, the cycle of revolt and repression was bound to recur.

Though similar in many crucial respects, the military institutions of Guatemala and El Salvador are distinguishable in more than name. While the latter's dependence on the United States has grown exponentially during the past decade, the former's has declined. When it was cut off by the Carter administration from its normal source of supply, it turned to Israel. The Galil assault rifle is now standard issue for combat troops. The Guatemalans run their own counterinsurgency program, produce counterinsurgency units that patrol aggressively in the most remote parts of the country, and in general display a degree of élan and competence superior to their Salvadoran counterparts.

A second distinguishing characteristic is the relative independence of the Guatemalan armed forces from the civilian Right. They seem less penetrable, tending, for instance, to prefer a monopoly of force rather than extensive sharing of the business of killing with paramilitary groups funded by the oligarchy. In addition, rather than being satisfied with payoffs and corruption, some senior officers have become landowners in their own right, following the lead of the old landholding class in using the power of the state to appropriate Indian land.

A third distinction is the extraordinary control, nothing short of totalitarian, that the military exercises throughout the countryside, but particularly in the highlands, over the rural population. Composed largely of unassimilated Indians—unlike El Salvador, where the bulk of the peasantry, whether pure Indian or of mixed race, have become Hispanicized—they live under conditions that have all the characteristics of foreign occupation in time of war. Many established villages are under the control of civilian commissioners, appointed by the military, who combine in their person executive, legislative, and judicial power. Outside of them, there is no court of last resort.

Model villages, into which villagers driven by the military out of zones of guerrilla activity have been herded, are prisons. No one leaves or enters without express permission. All over the country adult males are forced to spend many hours a week on antiguerrilla civil patrols. Failure to serve is treated as a confession of sympathy for the guerrillas. Under the *de facto* law of Guatemala, sympathy is a capital offense.

These were the conditions of life in Guatemala on January 14, 1986, when Marco Vinicio Cerezo took office as the country's first democratically elected civilian president since Julio César Méndez Montenegro (1966–1970). Cerezo, leader of the Christian Democrats, had survived assassination attempts during the regime of General Lucas Garcia by living like a fugitive barricaded in his own house. In light of the awful decimation of party members during the previous decade, while the parties of the Right functioned with almost complete impunity, Cerezo's overwhelming victory was both a surprise and a tremendous electoral mandate. Both his victory and the willingness of the armed forces to relinquish office, particularly to a man of the center, testified above all to the country's appalling economic conditions.

Between 1981 and 1986 per capita gross domestic product shrank 20.7%, substantially the largest economic contraction of any country in the region. (El Salvador, the next worse, had declined a mere 16.7%.) From 1983 to 1986 the value of real wages fell 46%. Government statistics indicate that from 1980 to 1984 there was a fivefold increase in unemployment, and since then the downward trend has continued. In 1986 the minister of labor declared that 51% of the country's work force is without permanent work.

Although—given the distribution of wealth and the military-controlled public sector's failure to ease inequality through transfer payments—the middle and lower classes bear the weight of depression disproportionately, even the landholding–business class has felt the need for relief. And officers in Guatemala, like their counterparts in other Latin American states, prefer to disassociate themselves from economic catastrophe. Apparently believing that one route to relief was foreign assistance and investment, the armed forces were willing to tolerate a government that would attract foreign support.

They were willing, it would seem, so long as they had guarantees that President Cerezo would not attempt to reduce their prerogatives. As an augury of Cerezo's room for maneuver, before relinquishing formal power to him the *de facto* government of General Mejía Víctores declared an amnesty intended to prevent prosecution of any past or present member of the security forces for any crimes whatsoever. The Argentine military had attempted the same ploy only to have President Raul Alfonsin brush it aside. But the Guatemalan armed forces, unlike the Argentine, were neither defeated nor conspicuously divided. Cerezo has not challenged this essay in self-exculpation.

A man of few illusions, he conceded at the outset that he had no more than 25% of the real power in the country. Developments since his inauguration suggest that, if anything, he may have been optimistic. Although freedom of speech has widened considerably and political killings have declined, the condition of human rights remains terrible. Killing is more selective, at least in the cities. But after the mass slaughter of the past 25 years, not only are there in an absolute sense far fewer activists to kill, in addition it takes only an occasional murder or disappearance to maintain a generalized sense of terror among the population. Furthermore, while the guerrillas have not been totally liquidated, their units and their capacity to mount substantial operations have declined radically and their threat to the established order rendered nugatory.

On the side of the armed forces, the institutions of terror and the sense of absolute freedom to employ it are unaffected by the transition to formal civilian rule. In apparent deference to the military institution's sensitivities, not only has Cerezo eschewed all efforts to prosecute anyone ever associated with the terror apparatus, he has as well shown little enthusiasm for efforts to determine the status of persons who "disappeared" (often before witnesses) under circumstances that strongly evidence their seizure by the security services. In addition to trying to close the door on the past, he has dragged his heels on measures that might be seen as inhibiting the discretion of the security forces in the future; for instance, he opposed legislation to establish a human rights ombudsman. More ominously, he has been reluctant to authorize inquiry into current cases of politically inspired killing or even to admit that such killings are occurring.

Both contemporary Guatemalan reality and President Cerezo's

sense of the precariousness of his position are illustrated by a case cited in the February 1987 report on human rights in Guatemala prepared jointly by the nongovernmental human rights organization Americas Watch and the British Parliamentary Human Rights Group. Celso Lopez Jop, a press secretary of Cerezo's own party, was tortured to death and left to die on December 1, 1986, in Mixco, a few miles outside Guatemala City. Local party leaders said that before dying, Lopez Jop declared that his torturers were members of the National Police in that town. The February 1987 report recounts:

> In an impromptu press conference, President Cerezo promised an investigation, but ventured that the case was "probably" not politically motivated and denied that it was meant to intimidate the Christian Democratic Party. A spokesman for the National Police agreed with President Cerezo that it was an act of common crime. Christian Democrat Party leaders, including Alfonso Cabrera, the President of the Congress, sharply disagreed with President Cerezo, calling the murder a "political crime" and demanding a special investigation. *La Hora* [a Guatemalan newspaper] reported on December 4 that 22 members of the Mixco police were questioned by investigators concerning the death and that they were temporarily removed from duty and substituted with other National Policy officers. At the time of this writing, there have been no further developments in the case, and to our knowledge, no one has been charged or prosecuted for the crime. (pp. 33 –34)

I think, however, that another recent case best illustrates the Kafkaesque condition of life and death in contemporary Guatemala:

> On January 25, 1987, a farm worker named Camilo Garcia Luis was abducted by unknown men in Guatemala City. His 22-year-old wife, Marta Odilia Raxjal-Sisinit, denounced the kidnapping to the BROE, the Special Operations Brigade of the National Police, at the 5th police precinct in Guatemala City. According to information from a family member, on January 27 the wife received a telegram from the BROE ordering her to come to the station or receive a fine of 50 quetzals. The same day, Marta Odilia Raxjal-Sisinit's mother was kidnapped from her home, where she lived with the young couple and their children, and disappeared. The women's bodies were found on January 30. The brother and son of the women, Mariano Raxjal-Sisinit, who denounced their disappearance and death, has since received death threats from the local Army intelligence unit in Chimaltenango. The whereabouts of Camilo Garcia Luis remain unknown.

President Cerezo's integrity and fundamental decency are not in question. On the contrary, I admire his courageous decision to remain in Guatemala at great personal risk during the Lucas years in the hope of eventually leading the country out of its prolonged nightmare. What is in question is the locus of real power in Guatemala and the nature of those who wield it. The president has, on the whole, continued to be candid in this respect. For instance, while he has advocated the return to Guatemala of the estimated 100,000 Indians who fled into Mexico to escape from the Guatemalan army, he has told church people in Mexico who have ministered to the refugees that at this point he could not guarantee their security. Nor is it necessary to rely on the president's words, acts, and omissions to grasp the real state of affairs. The generals have been no less candid. After Cerezo responded to a guerrilla proposal for negotiations by calling on them to lay down their arms and join the process of consolidating democracy, the minister of defense announced that reintegration of the guerrillas was not to be contemplated.

Given the character of the military institution and of the oligarchy (whose enthusiasm for democracy and human rights parallels that of their El Salvadoran neighbors), the crippling fear induced by two generations of repression, the weakness of intermediate institutions like labor unions, and the isolation and suspicion of the Indian majority, Cerezo's chances of building an authentic democracy are not bright. To say that the Reagan administration has done nothing to improve the odds he faces is to tell only half the truth. In addition, it has impaired them.

Having campaigned against Carter's so-called sacrifice of American preeminence on the altar of wimpish concern for human rights, the Reagan administration let the word go out to officers and oligarchs throughout Latin America that it would give them a new deal; that is to say, it would restore the old deal under which the United States guaranteed their survival. It also signaled its understanding of the criminal methods they found it useful to employ against the Left.

Suiting deed to word, the administration labored mightily to pry aid to the Guatemalan armed forces out of Congress. For that purpose, the president and his associates found it necessary to employ prodigies of mendacity, hailing each successive military regime as a champion of human rights, then retrospectively indicting it and themselves by describing the next ruling general as a vast improvement over his predecessor, now conceded to have been delinquent. And when, despite these labors of disinformation, Congress proved balky, the president evaded legislative restrictions by altering the definition of military items in order to permit transfer to the Guatemalan security forces of needed items like jeeps.

Against this historical backdrop, Cerezo was not well positioned to persuade the military that cooperation with him was a necessary condition of good relations with the executive power of the United States. And to the extent he sought to reduce the ferocity of the armed forces' repression of the Left, much less to draw the armed opposition out of the cold and into the political process, the generals could legitimately claim that his policies clashed with Ronald Reagan's preferences. Thus, Cerezo had to rely for leverage on his ability to attract aid from the U.S. Congress and the countries of Western Europe.

Having, by its prior acts, hampered Cerezo's effort to reduce both the barbarity and the hegemony of the military institution, the administration has, since his election, added new obstacles for him to vault. It has done so, presumably, not because of active hostility to a mildly reformist (in aspiration) civilian government but rather because it subordinates every other interest to the goal of destroying the government of Nicaragua.

With respect to the Nicaraguan conflict, President Cerezo follows a policy he labels "active neutrality." He will not join in the Reagan-sponsored coalition of Honduras and El Salvador (with Costa Rica during the presidential term of Luis Monge as an occasional and partial member), whose function, at least prior to September 1987, has been to frustrate all diplomatic solutions, and to create a felicitous environment for U.S. intervention by indicting

Nicaragua as a threat to regional peace. And he does encourage the search for a negotiated solution that would enhance the security of all Central American governments. In an effort to terminate Cerezo's independent diplomacy, the administration has broadly hinted to the Guatemalan armed forces that in return for a more accommodating foreign policy, Guatemala would receive much higher levels of military assistance. Thus we contribute to the expansion of democracy and human rights in the Uganda of the Western Hemisphere.

*Honduras.* I conclude this sketch of the national actors in Central America with a country whose present trajectory further illustrates the malign consequences of the policies we pursue in the high name of democracy.

On the one hand, Honduras is by far the most underdeveloped country in the region; indeed, its per capita income makes it the second poorest country, after Haiti, in all of Latin America. During this entire century it has been perceived, accurately, as the country that has managed the best possible fit with the term *banana republic*, not only or even primarily because of its dependence on this export crop, but rather because of its traditionally passive, if not sycophantic, relationship to the United States and the foreign interests controlling the growth and export of the banana crop.

On the other hand, by comparison with their counterparts in El Salvador, Guatemala, and Somoza's Nicaragua, the Honduran military seemed benign. It tolerated the development of trade unions among its very small working class and of peasant unions as well. It at least held dialogues with representatives of the poorer classes. It did not treat every effort to organize the lower classes as a threat to be liquidated forthwith. It even initiated a bit of land reform. And in the wake of revelations some years ago that the successor to United Fruit had bribed the then-president—a general, of course—in order to avoid the export tax on bananas, a group of younger officers forced their open-handed colleague to resign, seeming, thereby, to signal a break with customary complaisance in the face of official cupidity.

Prodded by the slowly expanding middle class, and pulled by the Carter administration, the armed forces finally resolved to restore civilian government. Full-fledged democracy was a bit much for them to swallow all at once. To assure election of someone with a due appreciation of military prerogatives, they manipulated the registration laws to hamstring the Christian Democratic Party, which they regarded as too reformist and uncontrollable. And they allowed the Liberal Party caudillo, Roberto Suazo Córdova, to assume office only after he had agreed not to exercise his constitutional power to replace officers whose commitment to civilian rule was doubtful. In spite of all that, everyone in the hemisphere who yearned to see the spread of democratic government felt some quickening of optimism about the future of Honduras.

That quickening soon slowed to a crawl. After Suazo Córdova took office, what became evident was that either most important decisions in Honduran society—particularly decisions about the budget and foreign and defense policy—were dictated by the senior officers of the military establishment (and/or by the U.S. ambassador) or, at best, they exercised a decisive veto. So civilian government functioned largely as a facade trying, or at least hoping, to acquire some volume.

When you take a country with a long tradition of profound psychological dependence on the United States, a country without any tradition of military subordination to civilian government, a country with a small middle class and a still essentially passive peasantry, a country that is miserably poor—when the United States takes such a country and pours resources directly into the hands of senior military officers, bypassing civilian authority, and concentrates its training programs on the officer corps and makes it clear that money will continue to flow as long as the civilian government does what it is told, the United States, however noble its intentions, is scooping away the ground on which the Honduran people might, under other circumstances, begin constructing a stable democracy.

The United States is doing more than that. The experience of civilian government created the will to resist *de facto* military rule and the effort, coordinated by the American Embassy, to convert Honduras into the land-based equivalent of an aircraft carrier from which U.S. forces could operate throughout Central America. Officers—warmly complicit in the process by which Honduras has been converted into a U.S. base for the conduct of semiclandestine war—together with right-wing business interests and, it is reported, local representatives of the Moonies, have all attempted to suppress critics. There have been beatings and some disappearances. Opponents have responded with a scattering of terrorist incidents. The society is polarizing as traditional tolerances and restraints shatter. Soon, if things continue on their present trajectory, not even the fragile tradition of dialogue will remain to commemorate a once-hopeful experiment.

## Policy in the National Interest or How Not to Shoot Yourself in the Foot while Shooting Others in the Head

As Richard Feinberg, vice-president of the Overseas Development Council, recently testified to the U.S. Senate, "Central America has economic promise. It has the climate, soils, hydro-electric potential, and technical expertise to develop diversified and dynamic economies. From 1950 until the late 1970s, Central America generated solid five percent growth rates, and could do so again." But first, he adds, "the United States must fashion a security policy which promotes peace—the *sine qua non* for economic development."*

The organic tie between the multidimensional American assault on Nicaragua and the region's economic depression is sug-

*Richard Feinberg, "Economic Assistance to Central America," statement before the Subcommittee on Western Hemisphere Affairs, Committee on Foreign Relations, United States Senate, March 25, 1987.

gested by two facts. First, economic depression in the region has worsened dramatically despite and coincident with a dramatic infusion of American aid. From 1981 to 1986 the United States poured $3.8 billion into the region (excluding Nicaragua and excluding as well the sort of military spending on locally supplied services that must have been quite large in El Salvador and particularly in Honduras). That amounts to roughly $865 per family of five, an impressive sum when you consider that the average annual income of such families in El Salvador and Honduras is $700. [For sources of data see United Nations Economic Commission for Latin America and the Caribbean (ECLA), *Preliminary Overview of the Latin American Economy 1986;* World Bank, *World Development Report 1986;* U.S. Agency for International Development, *Congressional Presentation FY 1986.*] The failure of foreign aid to stem economic contraction cannot be attributed solely to global economic conditions. In 1986 per capita GDP slipped in El Salvador, Guatemala, and Honduras despite substantial improvement in coffee and cotton prices, despite declining interest rates, and despite lower prices for oil. Nor has the Caribbean Basin Initiative, giving Central American exporters privileged access to U.S. markets, prevented a sustained and deepening depression.

In order to keep compliant governments afloat and compliant (in the Guatemalan case to sustain a government required to attract congressional support, which will be leveraged in an effort to obtain greater cooperation with Washington's grand design), the Reagan administration is requesting still more aid—a total of $1.1 billion for fiscal year 1987.

Precisely how does Reagan administration funding and support for war *à outrance* (against the government of Nicaragua and the insurgents in El Salvador) defeat the United States goal of promoting sustained economic growth with all its presumably beneficial political fallout? Feinberg identified five connections.

To begin with, the simultaneous promotion of insurgency (Nicaragua) and counterinsurgency (El Salvador) chills both local and foreign investors. The latter avoid involvement, while the former minimize their risks by exporting capital as it is earned. Thus, leaving aside the high levels of corruption in institutions, including the military, that will exercise direct or indirect control over the aid, the war-shaped incentive system guarantees that a good deal of it, rather than having a multiplier effect on the local economies, passes through them like a dose of salts and returns to developed world venues, such as Florida real estate and Zurich banks.

High aid levels, as Feinberg has noted, also have the unhappy consequence of allowing governments to postpone badly needed economic reforms: "[They] have permitted governments to maintain overvalued exchange rates, escape tax increases, and maintain inefficient capital markets" (p. 8). Normally, these governments would have had to seek support from the IMF and to accept, as a condition of support, precisely the reforms, conducive to long-term growth, that U.S. aid has enabled them to evade. Evasion pays short-term political dividends for the governments we have coaxed or are trying to coax into a *de facto* military alliance for war against Nicaragua. Thus, in pursuit of present obsessions, our policy constitutes a substantial down payment on long-term instability.

A third link between U.S. policy and economic contraction results from the historical interrelationship of all the Central American economies. The Central American Common Market was an important contributor to two decades of solid growth in the region. The economic isolation of Nicaragua coordinated with considerable success by Washington has contributed to the shrinkage of intraregional trade from $1.1 billion in 1980 to an estimated $370 million in 1986. Although refusing to accede to the boycott orchestrated in the White House, Costa Rica has not been able to avoid its consequences. For instance, Nicaragua's depleted currency reserves, in part a function of the boycott, have sharply cut its purchase of electrical energy from Costa Rica, which has traditionally relied on sale of its surplus to Nicaragua. "To avoid taking any actions that might even indirectly benefit Nicaragua," Feinberg has testified, "the Administration has deferred the Kissinger Commission's recommendations to revitalize the Common Market'' (p. 9).

Finally, it is important to recognize that U.S. insistence on making the overthrow of Nicaragua's government the centerpiece of its regional policy has forced the administration to act with little assistance from other democracies who could afford to contribute. They have been reluctant to support any regionwide effort regarding trade or aid that excludes Nicaragua.

The nub of the matter is that administration policy has contributed both to economic deterioration and to political developments inimical to the emergence of stable democratic governments anywhere in the region. That policy tends, moreover, to undermine the conditions of free government in Costa Rica. In other words, it manages at one and the same time to be expensive, squalid, and unsuccessful, except, perhaps, to the extent it should be credited with helping avert a guerrilla victory in El Salvador. Even that arguable attainment is problematical in that the Salvadoran armed forces blunted the so-called Final Offensive against them before the Reagan administration was well settled in office.

## The Realism of Benign Hegemony

To help ease the suffering of Central America's people and to promote the full range of U.S. interests in the area, we need to pursue a very different set of policies than those that have monopolized the decision-making agenda not simply for the past 7 years but for the 40 years that have elapsed since the end of World War II and the beginning of the cold war. Indeed, our optimum grand strategy may require us to jettison attitudes that have shaped American policy toward Latin America for more than a century. As I summarize in briefest possible compass the specific moves I would make, even at this late date, to rectify the consequences of current policy, I will clarify the assumptions that inform them.

American policy has been driven by the twinned objectives of

maintaining indisputably decisive influence in Latin America—
above all in the Caribbean Basin subregion—and preventing leftist
political parties and movements from obtaining even a share of
power, much less dominance, in any country. I would like to propose that U.S. interests would be better served by a somewhat different objective—namely, fostering stable representative
government and steady, broad-based economic growth in all regional states.

Representative governments presiding over economic systems
characterized by growth with equity will, of course, be more capable of resisting imperious demands from the United States. If influence is defined as the ability to compel the behavior of others, our
influence will have declined. But influence is only a means for
promoting larger ends. States continuously evolving along the lines
I have described will, because of material self-interest and the ideology naturally incident to such an evolution, interact with the
United States in ways that are mutually beneficial. They will not
require constant infusions of American aid. They will be good trading partners. Their environment will not generate powerful incentives for emigration. Their authority and resources will facilitate
their cooperation in suppressing transnational criminal activities.
Their political dependence on popular will and their economic dependence on interregional trade will discourage foreign adventures.
In short, they will be more useful neighbors than the sycophants
and satellites we seem to prefer.

However great our national effort to foster such political and
economic systems, because the countries of the region already
stand at very different points on the evolutionary scale and because
their natural and historical endowments vary greatly, we must expect very uneven results in the short and medium term. We lack the
will to impose the Japanese solution—that is, occupation and political reconstruction by *force majeure*. We lack the will because we
lack the incentive. The sort of evolution I describe, although beneficial to the U.S. national interest, is far from imperative. On the

contrary, despite its proximity, the subregion's importance exists largely in our minds.

The only development there that might have a substantial impact on our national security would be Soviet acceptance of an invitation to develop a base for one or another arm of its strategic forces. Why the Soviets would wish to deploy forces so far from the core of Soviet power and so close to the core of American power, forces that would attract a devastating preemptive strike in a time of high tension, I cannot easily imagine. Any prudent government would see that the risks outweigh any possible gain. In any event, we can preclude that contingency by military measures when and if it threatens to materialize. But having previously backed rhetoric with action, our credibility on the issue of Soviet strategic bases in the hemisphere is already so high that the probability of having to act again is extraordinarily low. That is why the "Soviet base" argument issue seems so fraudulent.

The nub of the matter is that sensible American concerns in the Caribbean Basin, as in the rest of Latin America, are not narrowly military and are not of such magnitude or so haunted by immediate and overwhelming risk as to justify some dramatic, costly, and risky initiative. What they do justify, as I have already suggested, are policies and attitudes rationally calculated to promote representative government and equitable growth. What they do not justify is sponsorship of unending civil war in El Salvador, proxy war against Nicaragua, the exercise of coercive diplomacy against civilian governments that do not wish to join our crusades, and the inflation of military establishments through the region. Standing those policies on their heads would be a healthy first step in the right direction.

A few countries in the region may already have political systems and elite ideologies able to alleviate progressively the misery of the poorer classes and to make them effective political and economic actors. But the majority have not reached that point. And their national experience suggests that only a coalition of the Center and the Left can overcome the determined opposition of right-wing officers and oligarchs. The United States has fiercely opposed such coalitions. It has, for instance, used the so-called American Institute for Free Labor Development (a cooperative venture of the CIA and the AFL-CIO) to divide existing unions or encourage the formation of new ones hostile to the Left and to the general idea of promoting the interests of the working class through direct participation in politics. The result has been weaker unions and weaker parties of reform.

Far more important to political developments in the area than any *particular* attempt to isolate and castrate the Left is the generalized hostility that oozes out of every nook and cranny of U.S. policy. From Truman through Reagan, Washington has used the entire range of its relations with Latin countries to express its hostility to the Left. Through our vastly influential military training programs, we have labored to wean Latin officers away from a definition of their mission emphasizing protection of the nation from external attack to one emphasizing an internal threat. In the process we have, of course, encouraged them to insinuate the military institution into the four corners of civil society. By emphasizing leftist "penetration" of unions, schools, universities, and the press, we have encouraged persecution of the very institutions whose vitality is essential to the construction and maintenance of representative government and to the generation of effective pressure for social reform.

But, Professor van den Haag will no doubt say, we have done these things because the Left is the enemy, whether or not it acts as the conscious agent of Soviet power. What the Left is, first of all, is a deceptive abstraction that has for close to a century been an integral element in the grand mosaic of conventional American demonology. If one limits the term to top leaders and the vanguard of activists operating today, one is still talking about hundreds of thousands of people. A group that large no doubt contains its fair share of thugs, sadists, psychopaths, and power trippers. Of course there is ample work for such people in the established security services.

Working for authoritarian governments is a good deal safer than working against them. During the past 80 years, most such governments have been governments of the Right. To be sure, the clandestine underground may have an infatuating romantic mystique the security services cannot readily match. In addition, modern Latin cultures tend to idealize service on behalf of the poor, so ambitious youth may choose the Left because it more neatly disguises ambition as idealism.

I do *not*, in short, claim that *all* persons who place themselves on the left of the political spectrum are humanitarians driven to violent revolution by the violence of governments defending the *status quo* and driven to anti-Americanism by U.S. collaboration with harsh governments and movements of the Right. I simply note, first, that the school of life in countries like El Salvador and Guatemala has imposed a regular dose of fraudulent elections, manipulation of the law to supplement the wealth of the rich and the poverty of the poor, and state-sponsored terrorism against proponents, however moderate, of social justice, as well as exemplary torture and assassination of uppity peasants and workers. And that in this school of hard knocks open to all without tuition, local representatives of the United States (businessmen, police and military advisors, intelligence agents, diplomats) have served during most of the postwar era as aiders and abettors. It logically follows, I would suppose, that anyone with the slightest social conscience and anyone from the deprived classes hoping to improve either their own position or the position of their class would be prepared by this schooling to surrender hope of nonviolent reform and to see the Soviet Union and Cuba as the only possible sources of practical assistance. In other words, one need not look to psychopathology or ideology to explain the orientation of the Latin hard Left. History will do.

In those few countries where it seemed possible to achieve reform through democratic processes, most of the Left has eschewed violence in favor of electoral and interest-group politics.

For decades, the Chilean Left played the game of democratic politics fairly, albeit in the end imprudently, in the sense of reaching for reforms that pushed a sizable segment of the middle class into an antidemocratic coalition with the upper-class elite and the military institution. When, in the early 1960s, centrist politicians in Venezuela—who had played the principal role in overthrowing a military dictator and had sought with some success to bring the trade union movement into the governing coalition—offered amnesty and freedom to participate in political competition without fear of extralegal harassment, many accepted the offer. One former leader is now a respected member of Congress.

There is no way to know what proportion of leftist activists would prefer an authoritarian politics and a state-managed economy. We have, after all, only one case in this hemisphere of a consolidated leftist regime and no case of such a regime evolving in anything other than an intensely threatening environment. Even the Reagan administration concedes that the Salvadoran political leaders who collaborated with the military coup-makers of 1979, and who left the government only after they found themselves unable to halt mass killing by the military, have a democratic vocation.

What I am proposing, in any event, is not U.S. support for leftist revolutions but rather support for Center–Left coalitions, in states where the Left has traditionally been persecuted, and concomitant withdrawal of the White House seal of approval from governments hostile to social reform and indifferent to the plight of the poor. All the tools of diplomacy, including regulation of public- and private-sector economic relations, should be applied to the end of encouraging reform-oriented coalitions and eliminating barriers to their success, above all inflated military establishments operating outside the law and exercising a veto over key political issues, including the size and composition of the national budget.

If, at the close of World War II, the U.S. policy elite had envisioned this country's proper role as that of catalyst and patron of political and social reform in the Caribbean Basin, the social forces released by economic growth, reinforced by American diplomacy, would have built for themselves open and stable and self-reforming political systems cooperating on terms of mutual respect along a wide spectrum of essentially common interests. But, for the United States to have played that role, it would have to have been a different country. Now, having itself gone through the school of hard knocks, both at home and abroad, it is a sufficiently different country to make the policy I propose an option politically and psychologically feasible for a president associated with the center of the Democratic Party.

To make a new start, however, we must come to terms with the world our actual postwar policy has helped to make. An authoritarian government of the Left rules Nicaragua, at least in part because we were reluctant to facilitate the removal of Somoza without assurance that the Left would be excluded from the succeeding political order. As I explained in detail earlier, our effort to destroy that government causes us to act in ways inimical to democracy and social reforms in neighboring countries. Therefore, the first step toward a policy more congruent with our enduring national interests in this area is a negotiated settlement along lines laid down by the Contadora mediators. In effect, we would be negotiating the neutralization of Nicaragua with on-site monitors supplementing national intelligence capabilities to assure compliance.*

As part of the settlement agreement, we should be able to obtain amnesty for the bulk of the Contra troops and for political figures who did not command Contra units complicit in crimes against the laws of war. However, in the case of Contra soldiers who do not wish to return, we should provide generous financial incentives for their resettlement in underpopulated Honduras.

Because a negotiated solution of the Salvadoran civil war is a precondition for economic recovery and benign political development in that country, and because, through the medium of the FDR-

---

*This was written just prior to the decision of the Central American presidents to adopt the peace plan developed by President Oscar Arias Sánchez of Costa Rica.

FMLN we could apply pressure on the Sandinista regime for a relaxation of restraints on the political opposition and strict adherence to the American Convention on Human Rights, we should call for simultaneous negotiation of all issues affecting the peace of Central America with full representation of all interested parties. The Contadora state would be asked to provide a venue for negotiations and to participate both as mediators and interested parties. In order to underscore the fact that its call for negotiations is intended to express concretely a fundamental shift in U.S. relations with Latin America, member states of Contadora's South American support group also should be invited. And since the renewal of economic growth in the region and the implementation of social and economic reform would be facilitated by contributions from Japan and the capitalist democracies of Western Europe, there is a case for drawing them into the discussions at an early point and thereby generating something close to an implicit commitment to help finance the developments the accords are intended to launch.

There is, I believe, a still stronger case for inviting Soviet participation. That case does not rest primarily on Soviet capacity to thwart the conclusion or implementation of satisfactory accords. It does not rest on that capacity because the Soviets do not have it. Nor does it rest on the possible utility of continued Soviet economic aid to Nicaragua and the initiation of assistance, however token, to a coalition government in El Salvador, assuming, as I do, that we have the raw influence over events in that country to force such a result. A minor advantage of Soviet participation is the possibility it would offer for testing the Soviet Union's will and capacity to play a constructive role in negotiations involving governments and movements that are at least friendly associates if not actual clients.

But the principal argument for considering Soviet participation is the opportunity to implicate the Soviet Union in a reordering of relations between a superpower and states falling within its traditional sphere of influence. Under the formula I am proposing for the Caribbean Basin, the United States would eschew unilateral recourse to force or the threat of force in order to maintain or impose ideologically congenial client regimes. The Latin states would commit themselves to eschew acts possibly inimical to U.S. security interest. Such acts would include military cooperation of any kind with an extrahemispheric power and the acquisition of nuclear weapons. The United States would, of course, remain free to use economic incentives and other diplomatic tools to influence the domestic and foreign policies of its neighbors.

Were we to move in this direction, we should frankly declare a sea change in American policy, advertise its precedental implications by labeling it the ''Finlandization'' of the American sphere of influence, and urge the Soviet Union to follow suit. In the era of *glasnost*, when the Soviet Union is beginning to reexamine through a less ideologically fixed lens than it has employed hitherto all policies that burden its economy, the precedent could contribute to a loosening of hitherto frozen conventional wisdom within the Kremlin on the best way to protect Soviet security interests in Eastern Europe. Any Eastern European side effects of Finlandization in the Western Hemisphere would be a nice bonus. But even if its consequences were contained within the hemisphere, Finlandization would significantly further the national interests of the United States and of the countries with whom we share this part of the globe.

The negotiations I envision would mark the end of childish muscle-flexing as a substitute for rational diplomacy, the end of the puerile compulsion to force those in Central America who disparage our traditional role as hemispheric hegemon to cry, ''Uncle!'' The bicentennial of the world's oldest operating constitutional order, whose survival testifies to our collective self-confidence, our tolerance of diversity, and our capacity for sophisticated adaptation, is a particularly appropriate time to put aside a last relic of our adolescence.

# CHAPTER 8

# Delusion and Reality Once More

## ERNEST VAN DEN HAAG

---

Although he promises to explain "Whither the National Interest," Professor Farer's discussion disregards the national interest in favor of clichés and diatribes about Central America's endemic tyrannies. It seems that all of them are owed to Ronald Reagan, president of the United States. The Reagan administration is accused of supporting these tyrannies, if not creating them, and somehow being guilty of whatever they are guilty of—as though, before the Reagan administration, there was but peaceful and idyllic democracy in Latin America and as though, without Reagan, there would be no Central American tyrannies. Clio is loved by Professor Farer where convenient, and forgotten when her actions do not fit his ideological preconceptions. No way to treat a nice girl. Serious evidence is not presented for the Reagan sins, unless overblown rhetoric counts as argument.

In all this there is no glimmer of realism. Bad as it was, the Russian Czar's regime was certainly better than that of his Bolshevist successors. Still, the United States has to deal with the Soviets, simply because they hold power, however much they have violated all human rights and common decency for more than 60 years. So with Central American regimes. We must deal with power holders, however much we would prefer to deal with democrats, or, at least, decent people.

Professor Farer can do better than offering clichés. His summary of my views (p. 151) is fair, if incomplete. But he cannot restrain himself from adding, "It is not quite clear to me what Professor van den Haag feels about the costs [of supporting the Contras] to the Nicaraguan people," only to assert, inconsistently, a few lines below that "to the true believer in *realpolitik*"—he means me—"[the human costs] are irrelevant." So he does presume to know what I feel about these costs. He is wrong, of course. The difference between us is not that he minds these human costs and that I don't. Rather, he feels that we should not encourage Nicaraguans to defend themselves against Communism, or help them. By supporting them we somehow cause the "cost" and "prolong poverty." I feel that the Contras are Nicaragua's only hope of not "prolonging poverty" and not being swallowed by the totalitarian Sandinistas. The human costs of not fighting exceed the human costs of fighting. Wars, civil or not, always have a human cost. But sometimes there is no other way of defending justice and democracy. Neither comes cheap when threatened by Communism. Poverty has been prolonged in the Soviet Union precisely because the Communists were allowed to impose their dictatorship. This fate threatens Nicaragua and with it all the Communist evils—lack of freedom and human rights, imprisonment, torture.

Professor Farer feels that without the Contras, whom we should not support, the Sandinistas, although "not paragons," would be better than "the military masters of El Salvador and Guatemala." I think the word *Cuba* is sufficient refutation for this apologetic fantasy. The consolidation of the Sandinistas would leave the country bereft of any hope for democracy in the foreseeable future. Communist regimes do not go peacefully and cannot be reformed.

I do not know what to make of incidental allegations such as "Contragate has now revealed...[that the American] executive branch...slides facilely into erosion of Constitutional restraints." (Watch that metaphor!) I was under the impression that Congress is investigating possible Constitutional violations by the executive. As

I am writing in response to Farer, no one in the executive branch has been indicted in this matter, let alone convicted. Aren't the as-yet-unconvicted persons innocent until proven guilty?

Professor Farer complains that in pressing what it sees as our national interest in Nicaragua, the executive "generates [moral] costs by overstepping the limits of Constitutional power." But I doubt that President Reagan has done so in ways that could be remotely compared to the Constitutional overstepping of his predecessors from Lincoln to Franklin Delano Roosevelt. Nor do I seeany substance in the alleged Sandinista "conviction" that the United States would "move against any program of egalitarian social reform." This is Sandinista propaganda to which Farer appears remarkably receptive. He is welcome to it. It is modeled on Soviet propaganda. The egalitarian argument has been used by the Soviets since Lenin's time. The fact is that we do, and should, support those who oppose the Communist (Sandinista) consolidation in Nicaragua, both for the sake of the people of Nicaragua and because the implantation of a second Soviet ally in our neighborhood is too dangerous to ignore. Whether Nicaragua has an egalitarian social order or not is not relevant to our policy, although we would like the Nicaraguans to decide for themselves by free and peaceful elections, which the Sandinistas have not permitted. Incidentally, there is no indication that the Sandinistas are any more egalitarian than the Soviets or the Cubans. Comforts and power are distributed as unequally as ever. The comandantes and their hangers-on have both, the rest neither. Professor Farer, unsurprisingly, confuses the rhetoric with the facts.

Indeed, Professor Farer makes rather free with the facts. He writes: "governments of the Left are by their nature uncooperative [with us]...hence, the preservation of conservative governments" is our goal. The government of El Salvador is Socialist (although opposed to Communist guerrillas taking over) and cooperative. France has a Socialist president and, until a year ago, a Socialist government. Both were more cooperative than the previous Conservative government. The Socialist government of Germany was as cooperative as the current conservative government. So is the Socialist government of Spain. But these are democratic leftists. Professor Farer obviously refers to pro-Communist governments when he writes of "governments of the Left." These indeed prefer to cooperate with the Soviet Union, as Cuba and the Sandinistas do, not pro-leftist but because pro-Soviet.

Professor Farer would have been more realistic if he pointed out that Central American leftists on the whole are hostile to the United States, not because of their leftism, or of American opposition to it, but because of their pro-Soviet stance, and because of fear, resentment, and envy of a neighbor that has a well-ordered and stable social system, and a prosperous economy—something no Central American government has achieved except for Costa Rica. Of course, we do have an interest in having cooperative governments (Left or Right) abroad. Professor Farer, as though revealing how mean we are, suggests that we define cooperativeness as "agreement with Washington's definition of problems and Washington's solution." Well, cooperativeness is based on a common definition and solution for the problems one cooperates on. Is that wrong?—or, as Farer writes, "servile"?

Farer tells us that we need bases, or force supplements, in the Western Hemisphere only if we want "a capability to determine the outcomes of civil wars." Not so. We need military capability to help defend Western Hemisphere states against Cuban, and now Nicaraguan, attacks. These two small states have the largest military forces in the Caribbean. Farer goes on to pooh-pooh the possible cooperation of the Sandinistas with the Soviet Union. It is, he says, unlikely, but if it does happen it is because we are so nasty to those poor Sandinistas. Far from it. We helped topple Somoza (subsequently murdered). He was a comparatively mild dictator, more tolerant of opposition than the Sandinistas, just as, at first, we welcomed Castro. (American policy has always been naive and vulnerable to leftist propaganda. Our government habitually is almost as gullible as Professor Farer. The Reagan administration is the exception, which is what makes Farer so angry. At any rate, we subsidized both Castro and the Sandinistas until their true colors became obvious.) Castro admitted later that he always had been a pro-Soviet Communist (embarrassing his admirers at *The New York Times*, who had stoutly maintained, as Professor Farer does for the Sandinistas, that it was only our refusal to finance him that drove Castro into the Soviet embrace). Castro allowed the Soviet Union to park missiles in Cuba. His armies still fight in support of Communist regimes in Africa. Yet Professor Farer (without embarrassment!) tells us that the Sandinistas never would accept Soviet help were it not for our nastiness. Wishfulness can interfere with common sense.

"Any jury," Farer writes, must return a verdict of "not proven" about the United States expectations of Sandinista loyalty to the Soviet Union. Foreign policy is not decided by a jury trial, which can find the accused guilty only if there is proof beyond a reasonable doubt. Juries deal with past acts. Foreign policy deals with expectations about the future. They are based on past experience (such as those with Cuba) but cannot be proved correct beyond a reasonable doubt until it is too late to do anything. We should have acted on our suspicions about Castro and the Sandinistas earlier on, before they seized total power. Unfortunately, our decision makers waited for more proof—which is why Castro and the Sandinistas were able to gain and keep power.

In his attempt to apologize for Latin totalitarians by saying they are no worse than others, Professor Farer does not hesitate to engage in anachronistic comparisons. "It was," he writes, "conservative governments" that sold blacks into slavery "no less heartless" than the actions of "Hitler and Stalin." The selling was done largely by Arabs and by fellow blacks. The conservative governments of Europe actually did prevent their citizens from keeping slaves. Our government, though hardly conservative, did not. Slavery had existed since antiquity. It hardly was invented by "conservatives,'' by reactionary ancient Egyptians, Greeks, and Romans. The whole notion of pretending that slavery was somehow a "conservative" idea is absurd. The comparison with Hitler's concentration camps merely shows that Professor Farer lacks a sense of proportion. Slaves were enslaved, not intentionally killed, as the black population of the United States attests. They were exploited and often mistreated, but not systematically worked to death or killed as the Jews were. Stalin's victims were simply starved to death. The slaves were not. Their descendants are with us.

Professor Farer also has some vague but original economic theories, which he reveals in discussing migration. Latins are poor, he writes, because the "upper classes ... manipulate exchange rates and tariffs so as to reduce the cost of imported labor-saving technology." In other words low (or absent) tariffs for cost-reducing machinery are bad. I cannot think of any economist who would allow a sophomore to get away with that bizarre notion. The lower the cost of labor-saving machinery, the higher the standard of living.

"The Reagan administration's effort to destroy the leftist insurgency in El Salvador and the leftist government of Nicaragua does not pass this test [of social reform]," Farer writes. He does not mention that the El Salvador insurgents are Communists ("leftist" is more acceptable) and have been shown to have no popular support in elections generally declared fair by American observers, elections that took place despite the sabotage and the threats of the Communists. The Sandinistas too are totalitarians.

Farer ignores the obvious: What Latin America needs most is the institution of a genuine free market. Unfortunately, both leftist and rightist governments oppose it. They prefer to run the economy themselves as a source of patronage. We do not sufficiently urge a free market, and indeed, our economic help often has supported state socialism. The lack of free markets, the persistence of an archaic feudalist economy is among the many causes of Latin poverty. It will no more be abolished by Sandinistas than it was abolished by the Soviets. Efficiency has nowhere been part of socialism. Nor has equality, in practice, despite the ideology. Here again, Farer makes rather free with history. Poverty, he writes, and inequality undermine government stability. Not so. Caste systems have been stable for millennia, despite great masses of impoverished outcasts, and immense inequalities of prestige, power, or income. The Soviet Union is quite stable, as is India, despite great inequalities in income, power, and prestige. I don't like poverty or inequality any better than Farer does—but the effects of either on political stability depend on cultural factors. Professor Farer simply assumes that whatever is bad—e.g., poverty—must also lead to instability and revolutionary fervor. This is simplistic in conception and false in reality.

Professor Farer writes that inequality "makes it possible to see lower-class misery as a result not of an absolute insufficiency of national wealth but rather of a system of political economy that distributes it." Cagily he does not tell us whether he thinks the perception correct. It is not. If the unequal income or wealth in Central America were redistributed, as Farer elsewhere advocates, "lower-class misery" would not be relieved, since the wealth of the few rich would not suffice to make a perceptible difference for the many poor. Of course, this has been the Communist experience everywhere; it can be easily predicted on the basis of arithmetic. The truth is that, despite misperception and the propaganda to which Professor Farer is not immune, the existing national wealth of any country is insufficient, however distributed, to relieve poverty.

Why is redistribution unhelpful? Not that Latin America lacks natural resources. Rather, its economic system is unproductive, not because of inequality but largely because it rests on the very conceptions Professor Farer appears to advocate. To begin with, forceful threats of redistribution do not encourage investment. Further, large government intervention in the economy, lack of free markets, dependence on foreign aid, large government monopolies staffed by ex-generals and politicians without business experience, too much government regulation, and, as unavoidable consequence, pervasive corruption of the swollen bureaucracy—all these things keep countries poor. Not least, the instability and arbitrariness of governments make investment scarce. Deplorable as this is, Latin poverty is not what causes instability; a good case could be made for the reverse proposition. Poverty is largely due to the lack of a free market. The leftist revolutions Professor Farer favors, which he thinks will improve matters, tend to further institutionalize the very poverty and inequality they are supposed to remedy.

Professor Farer writes that the United States "has behaved in ways tending to erode political order in Colombia, Mexico, Panama, and Venezuela." No evidence is offered. I think the contention is wholly untrue, if Farer refers to the last 50 years. The political order in Mexico is dictatorial, corrupt, and inefficient. It keeps Mexicans in poverty and wastes the country's natural resources. Yet there is little we can do about it. And we certainly did not bring it about. I wish Professor Farer were right, and we could help to change the Mexican system of government. But I do not see how it can be done.

We have bolstered—for better or for worse—Panama's political order by ceding the Panama Canal to its government. It is not an appetizing order, but again there is little we can do about it. Colombia is largely run by drug dealers—and we have not been able to do anything about it. I have no idea to what Professor Farer refers when he writes that we are "tending to erode the political order" in these countries, including Venezuela. I wish we could.

Farer goes on, noting that "if the administration follows its instincts and makes war against Nicaragua" it will irk our Latin friends. I thought Professor Farer was to write about Central America, not about his fantasies. There is no reason to assume that this administration has "instincts" that will lead it to go to war against Nicaragua. Our support of the Contras is meant to avoid any need for doing so. There is no more likelihood of this, or of any administration planning a war against Nicaragua than one against Cuba, although we may well be prepared, or should be, to support Nicaraguans or Cubans fighting their respective dictatorships.

I find some odd remarks even in Professor Farer's comparatively dispassionate discussion of Costa Rica. He feels that Costa Rica is pushed by Reagan's policies toward upgrading its barely existing military capacity. Couldn't it be the existence of neighboring totalitarian Nicaragua, with its huge army (which can hardly be explained by its civil war alone), that causes the Costa Ricans to start worrying about self-defense? Somoza was no threat and had but small forces. The Sandinistas are a threat and have a huge army. Censoriously, Farer adds that the newly bolstered Costa Rican Civil Guard was used to "break up a hospital workers' strike." He tells us nothing about that strike (not where, when, why). I think that no such strike should ever be allowed. No one is compelled to work in a hospital. But everyone who does assumes a responsibility to the helpless patients not to disrupt their care by striking. Professor Farer does not tell the reader whether the hospital strike in Costa Rica was legal. I doubt it. It surely should be broken up by all available means. Incidentally, are any strikes allowed in Nicaragua? Cuba?

Farer goes on to complain that "the costs of austerity in Costa Rica were borne by the lower classes." Could it be otherwise? A reduction of consumption (which is what Farer means by "the cost of austerity") by the upper classes would not be significant for the economy. It would make no difference, even in the United States, if the rich were to reduce their consumption by 20%. (A reduction of saving or investment I presume even Farer realizes would be disastrous.) But if the "lower classes" reduce their consumption by only 5%, total consumption would be reduced by at least 4.5%. Wherefore the costs of austerity are unavoidably borne by the "lower classes" regardless of Professor Farer's wishes and fantasies. (Incidentally, this is the case regardless of whether the country is capitalist, Socialist, or Communist.)

Professor Farer concludes his summary of conditions in Costa Rica by mentioning in passing that the "public sector...employs close to 20% of the work force." He does not connect this with the strangulation of development but tells us that in some mysterious and unexplained way "U.S. strategy for and operation in Central America...inhibit Costa Rican efforts...to shrink...the public sector...." No evidence whatever is presented for this allegedUnited States policy, which would be contrary to everything we try to accomplish in Central America. Nor for Farer's conclusion: "If our principal goal were a Central America populated by stable democracies, we would be going about it in an ass-backward way." Assertions, even when repeated *ad nauseam*, do not amount to evidence, or even to argument.

In discussing El Salvador Professor Farer really lets go. It is a terrible country with a terrible social system and it is all our fault. The people (good) tried to overthrow the government (bad), which "butchered the guerrillas" (i.e., fought against them), who consisted of "peasant, largely Indian, masses." Of course, the guerrillas are nice (after all they are "peasant masses" and Indian to boot). They never "butcher" anyone. Government casualties must be due to the suicidal tendencies of government soldiers.

There is a civil war in El Salvador, with plenty of atrocities on all sides. It was started and is continued by a motley group of guerrillas, dominated by Communists, who explicitly reject elections and democracy as instruments of reform. Farer asks, "if with their steadily growing firing power [government troops] succeed in destroying effective opposition [Farer's odd name for Communist guerrillas], will they accept the...contraction in their size justified by the loss of a credible internal threat?" I think the troops are busy bringing about the "loss of the credible internal threat" that Professor Farer seems to fear. Demobilization after victory no doubt will bring problems, but so far I worry about bringing about the victory, not the ensuing demobilization. I find Farer's reasoning odd, to say the least. As odd as his complaint that the right has "pressured President Duarte to reduce the public sector's role in the economy and to permit the reestablishment of private banks." Right on, I say. Professor Farer thinks "reliance on the private sector to build a stable democratic and just society is anomalous." I think it is the only way to get it.

Whatever is wrong in El Salvador in Professor Farer's view is President Reagan's fault. Never mind that the Central American states usually were miserable dictatorships before Reagan was born; never mind that he didn't invent poverty, corruption, or guerrillas. It must be his fault, for, after all, otherwise Professor Farer would have to seriously analyze why Central America is as undeveloped, unfree, and inefficient as it is. Political slogans are easier—although, unlike Farer, I find them less satisfying.

Farer concludes his depiction of El Salvador by writing that the civil war there can be ended only by negotiation. He ignores the well-established fact that Communists will not share power except to take it over (as in Nicaragua). The lack of successful negotiations—you guessed it—is Reagan's fault. Anyway, if Farer does not think that the civil war could end with a government victory, why did he worry about the demobilization of government troops after victory? And why does he tell us that "stable democracy" could be produced by concessions to, and negotiations with, the Left? Is there any case in which Communists have produced, or even tolerated, a "stable democracy"?

On Guatemala Farer outdoes himself. It is "the Uganda of Latin America." (Uganda was peaceful and prosperous under the British. Was Guatemala ever? We are not told.) It is all our fault as usual. The military are in control in Guatemala (and almost always have been) and they have effectively suppressed all rebellions. The democratically elected president has limited power and the military disregard civil rights. All this is far from ideal, although probably better than the leftist dictatorship that is the effective alternative. The economy is not doing well and the government has failed "to ease inequality through transfer payments," i.e., redistributive taxes. (Professor Farer likes euphemisms.) And no one told him that redistributive taxes everywhere have made matters worse, leading to declining production and more poverty.* Poverty is not relieved through redistribution (although envy may be) but, exclusively, through more production.

The elected president of Guatemala has encouraged the search for a negotiated solution in Nicaragua, but we, "in an effort to terminate Cerezo's independent diplomacy," have "broadly hinted to the Guatemalan armed forces" that without Cerezo's diplomacy "Guatemala would receive more military assistance. So we contribute to the expansion of democracy...." I don't think that any of this is any more than fantasy. And why would a promise of more military support for Guatemala (and pressure against its Nicaraguan diplomatic initiatives) be inconsistent with the expansion of democracy? Would the victory of Guatemalan guerrillas help?

The United States is far more prosperous and far more powerful than all the Central American, indeed, all the Latin American countries together. This fact unavoidably looms over our relations with the rest of the hemisphere. Historically the United States has been only a little more shy in using its preponderant power to pursue its interests than the European powers were when they held Latin American countries as colonies. But, whereas the Spanish and Portuguese were the settlers of the Latin colonies, we were not. And Americans predominantly are of non-Latin stock, whereas at least Central America's upper classes tend to be Spanish or Portuguese, although, by now, much Indian and black blood has been added, and many non-Iberians—Germans, Italians, Japanese, to mention a few—have become part of the population.

Unavoidably, cultural differences and the great difference in power and prosperity, as well as the history of the American role in Central America, have led to a very ambivalent relationship. Central Americans resent, despise, and, above all, envy the United

---

*Sweden may be the exception that proves the rule, but I know too little about it to be certain.

States. They tend to attribute all their innumerable ills to the United States, as does Professor Farer. Any corruption, cruelty, poverty, misgovernment is blamed on the United States. Things are simpler that way, as Professor Farer too has found. Unfortunately, it also means that Central Americans do not face their real problems. It is easier to blame it all on Uncle Sam.

Is there even a kernel of truth in all this? I think not. To be sure, there are many sins that historically can be blamed on us. We have paid little heed to Latin independence in the past. But even when we sent the marines, our occupation, though scarcely licit, was neither cruel nor oppressive. The average citizen probably was better off with American occupation than he was with his native government. This is not to justify the occupation but simply to state a fact.

President Franklin Delano Roosevelt in effect renounced the crude imperialism that had characterized our relations with Central America. Since his time, although we often supported pro-American factions in the civil strife that has characterized so much of Central American history, we rarely have intervened directly. Although Latin politicians like to blame the United States for the poverty of the countries they govern, in fact that poverty is quite native, and has been ameliorated by United States investments and trade. The reason that Central America is not as successful as, say, South Korea or Singapore, let alone Japan, is not U.S. "exploitation" but rather the heritage of oligarchy, stupid and corrupt government, and harebrained economic policies that was left to Central American countries by the colonizers. Particularly since the Second World War, the main U.S. role has been to grant and lend money to Latin American countries. Most of that money will never be repaid. Unfortunately, it did little to help the recipient countries either. It was wasted by their governments, which have a tendency not only to enrich themselves but also to mismanage the economy in the process. Resources tend to be government-owned and mismanaged. Private initiative is stifled. Workers are exploited both by the government and by their own unions, and now, finally, by leftist guerrillas. It is simple to blame the United States. But it is neither truthful nor helpful.

Indeed, beyond preventing the expansion of Communist influence, there is little we can do. Even in trying to resist communism we have not done overwhelmingly well, as Cuba, El Salvador, and Nicaragua show. About corruption, inefficiency, dictatorship, army dominance, and mismanagement there is hardly anything we can do.

Yet a bad government can always be replaced by a worse one, as shown by Castro and the Sandinistas. We should have learned as much from the Soviet Union. Or, later, Cuba. But as Professor Farer demonstrates, many of us are unwilling to learn from history, when learning would mean giving up cherished dreams, hates, and Utopian constructs.

The ills of Central America will have to be cured by endogenous Central America reform, difficult as it is. Replacement of military dictators by leftist and Communist guerrillas will only make matters worse and more permanent. Rightist dictatorships can yield to reform, as Spain, Portugal, Greece, Argentina, Uruguay, and Brazil show. When they are overthrown by violence, they tend to be replaced by Communist dictatorships, as Cuba, Nicaragua, and the Soviet Union (not to speak of Vietnam) also show.

Professor Farer laments, above all, the cruelty of Latin civil wars, and of military suppression of guerrillas in Central America. Discounting his odd reasoning (it is all our fault) and his one-sidedness (the cruelty is all on the side of the military, the guerrillas are just nice people, unless it is in Nicaragua, where the military are nice—since they fight for the Sandinistas—and the guerrillas [Contras] are nasty, since they are pro-American), Farer is right. The cruelties on both sides are atrocious.

In most Central American countries the judiciary is neither powerful, nor efficient, nor independent. It follows that the major protection against crime, political or otherwise, is in the hands of the armed forces. The elected government (if there is one) cannot act against the military and has little control over it and, therefore, over the country as a whole. Hence, the abuses of military power are as frequent as the uses.

In fairness it must be said—though it cannot be proved beyond a reasonable doubt—that Argentina, Chile, Uruguay, El Salvador, perhaps even Brazil might well have become Communist dictatorships were it not for the activities of the military forces in suppressing leftist terrorism. But the counterterror was not pretty. And the military used it to try to eliminate whatever and whoever displeased them. Still, the reintroduction of democracy would be impossible had the leftist terror not been defeated—by the military. The task now is to try to reform and control it. It is a daunting task, and it can be accomplished only by Central America itself. We may be able to prevent the export of communism—but we are not able to export democracy, honesty, or efficiency.

# V

# CONCLUSIONS

CHAPTER 9

# Peace without Totalitarianism

## ERNEST VAN DEN HAAG

Central America is an important part of the world, and Latin America as a whole is immensely important. Industrial development, distorted and retarded by foolish and exploitative governments, cannot be delayed much longer. As it proceeds, the importance of Latin America will become obvious. Countries such as Brazil and Argentina possess immense, if as yet undeveloped, resources. So do the smaller Central American republics. It is true that much has been expected for a long time of Brazil and Argentina and of Central America, and so far very little has come to pass. Instability and silly government policies have made it impossible so far for these countries to develop as the United States has. There is a lack of free markets, of incentive, of education. Investment lags because investors feel that their capital may be confiscated by the government or destroyed by guerrillas. But if governments become democratic, common sense will prevail. And Latin countries are slowly—all too slowly—getting rid of their dictatorships and moving toward democracy. The transition is difficult and fitful, but the trend is readily discerned.

Democratization is endangered mainly by the threat of communism. Communists, disguising themselves as radical democrats to fool the naïve, tend to infiltrate the forces of democracy. They may capture power from inexperienced democrats hypnotized by the danger from rightist dictatorships that they fought in the past. This happened in Nicaragua. Even the Soviet regime was instituted not by overthrowing the czar—that was done by the democratic opposition—but by overthrowing the only democratic government Russia ever had. It was weak and did not understand the threat of Communism until it was too late.

We must learn from history, our common experience. Its lesson is that, in Latin America, the opportunity for democracy—and therewith for development, human rights, security, and prosperity—depends on defeating the Communists, be it in El Salvador, Peru, Nicaragua, or anywhere else. Communists often have drawn strength from the injustices and the corruption of rightist dictatorships. We should not blindly support them as a bulwark. As a matter of fact, we do not, as the Philippines, Haiti, or Santo Domingo show, not to speak of Spain, Greece, Portugal. Yet we cannot overthrow dictators. This can be done only by the residents of the country they rule. (Grenada was an exception, not a paradigm.) We may support Contras, as we do in Nicaragua, when the Soviets support their fellow Communists. But, in the main, democracy cannot be exported. Let me now summarize some of the matters we have been discussing.

There is first international law, in which Professor Farer puts more faith than I do. (Faith is "the evidence of things not seen." In political matters, that is not the relevant kind of evidence.) I have drawn attention to the fact that, where it matters, international law cannot be enforced. It depends on voluntary acceptance by independent nations. But, almost by definition, laws that depend entirely on voluntary compliance are not laws. A law that does not compel persons to act according to their legal obligations, or punish those who break it, is scarcely a law. It is merely an exhortation, a suggestion. Hence, international law—a series of customs, treaties, and conventions voluntarily subscribed to and honored sometimes, and sometimes not—is scarcely law. A nation that follows international law, when it is inconsistent with the national interest, will find that international law cannot protect it against other nations that ignore it. This certainly is one matter on which Professor Farer and I disagreed.

Another matter is the role of human rights. Professor Farer insisted throughout that many governments with which we have amiable relations are less than perfect democracies and, in his view, are guilty of human rights violations. I think this is true, even though he exaggerates the degree of our support and minimizes human rights violations committed by leftist guerrillas. But I do not think that we can transform these countries into democracies by waving a magic wand. Most of Central America has been governed undemocratically, inefficiently, and corruptly by different casts of dictators for a long time. Often the military hold the major power in Central America and exercise it directly or indirectly, but, usually, badly. However, displaying hostility to these governments would not change them. Contrary to many assertions, they do not depend sufficiently on us to make it possible to change their behavior by withdrawing support. And, as Nicaragua has shown (and Cuba before it), the alternative may be a Communist government no more democratic or efficient, no less corrupt or violative of human rights, while far more hostile to us and pro-Soviet to boot.

Foreign policy is not like a party to which we invite only people we like. We must protect our security and our interests by associating with many governments we would prefer to be different. That is why we have relations with the Soviet Union (which we supported against Hitler) and other Communist dictatorships, and why we have relations with right-wing dictators as well, even when their human rights record is bad. Actually, by having such relations we have been able to improve somewhat the human rights situation in the Soviet Union, Poland, and Chile—though there is room for much more improvement.

The human rights record in Communist countries—improved since Stalin's time but still bad—is entirely the responsibility of their governments. In most Central American countries responsibility is more diffuse because power is. Although run as dictatorships, these countries are not totalitarian. The power of the political authorities over the military is limited. The military itself often is divided. When reputed Communists in El Salvador are murdered by rightist groups, when "death squads" take the law into their own hands, they often are enabled to do so by the weakness of the government, which finds it impossible to impose its authority on warring left and right factions and guerrillas. Nothing favorable would be achieved in such cases by further weakening a government that is unable to prevent human rights violations. (But the situation is different in each country.)

The aim of our foreign policy must be, in the first place, to provide for our security by preventing the expansion of pro-Soviet forces, and, in Central America, to enforce the Monroe Doctrine. We can support human rights, but basically they can be instituted only by the citizens of the country in which they are to prevail. We cannot remove the Soviet government. We can probably prevent the consolidation of a Communist government in Nicaragua. We allowed it to consolidate itself in Cuba. We originally supported the Sandinistas, as we did Castro. We need not continue or repeat our mistakes.

CHAPTER 10

# Let's Not Snatch Endless War from the Jaws of an Imperfect Peace

## TOM J. FARER

For all its considerable virtues, the debate format as a means of clarifying volatile contemporary issues has certain potential defects. Since the participants must await each other's thrusts, by the time they have finished with the subject as it was when they began, it may have shifted in ways demanding further comment. That is one problem. A second is the tendency of prolonged and intense debate shifting rapidly among the subject's various facets to obscure one's overall position; readers may be left in the position of the blind wise men holding different parts of the elephant's anatomy and trying without communication among themselves to determine what the beast looks like. It seems to us that a brief final statement might obviate these difficulties.

*August 1987: The context of policy.* My opening statement dates from the period 1983–1984. Since that time, the Reagan administration has armed, trained, and, arguably, institutionalized the Contra armed forces to the point where they may not melt away quickly in the event Congress cuts off aid as part of a multinational accord that, in effect, commits all interested parties to recognize the legitimacy of existing governments and to refrain from supporting insurgents. Enhanced capacities, demands in the United States for a demonstration of efficacy, and pressure from Honduras to leave have led to a situation where the bulk of Contra troops now appear to be inside Nicaragua. The result is a much higher level of violence in rural areas. As many people on both sides of the debate predicted, intensification of the conflict has coincided with imposition by the Sandinista government of harsher contraints on political activity in particular and dissent in general,* and with graver violations of human rights by that government as well as by the Contras.

Professor van den Haag presumably believes that the conflict simply provides a convenient excuse for the Sandinistas to accelerate movement along the road to full-scale totalitarian government, which they intended to follow in any event. I remain agnostic about their alleged aspirations and convinced that, whatever their aspirations, for all the reasons elaborated in my opening statement, the United States and allied democracies can best thwart that tendency by nonviolent means. And, despite the periodic reshuffling of the Contras' political superstructure, I am unable to convince myself that a Contra victory, made possible by direct U.S. military intervention, is likely to result in the democratization of Nicaragua.

The Sandinista leadership and its supporters still seem to constitute a substantial portion of the population. (From all accounts, a majority appear acquiescent—that is, unenthusiastic about the government while regarding the Contras as an unappealing alternative.) If driven from government, they would remain so grave a threat to the new regime that it would inevitably attempt to liquidate them. Moreover, given the need to consolidate its authority by rewarding its own soldiers and conciliating powerful interests from the old *status quo*, a counterrevolutionary government would also use its coercive powers to displace employees of governmental and quasi-governmental institutions at all levels, as well as those peasants who secured land under the Sandinistas. Human-rights-loving democrats will not thrive in an era of Thermidorian reaction.

---

*Suddenly reversed since the Central American presidents, in September 1987, signed the peace proposal of Costa Rican President Oscar Arias Sánchez.

In brief, then, I do not believe that the developments enumerated above have undermined the objections I have raised to existing policy. They do, however, complicate implementation of the alternative approach to the Nicaraguan problem that I sketched at the outset of this exchange of views and that I will recapitulate as soon as I add a word about conditions in El Salvador.

This second piece of the Central American puzzle seems to have arrived at an awful stalemate. While the level of indiscriminate slaughter has fallen dramatically, the elements that at the close of the 1970s turned this country into an abattoir seem to be fundamentally unaltered.

The government lacks the power and the means—possibly the will as well—either to complete the process of social and economic reform initiated at the beginning of the decade or to conceive and launch a new one. The armed forces remain a law unto themselves. Indeed, given the state of the legal system, one could fairly say that the law still does not rule over anyone in El Salvador. The powerless majority remain subject to the often conflicting whims of those who have or control guns.

Leaders of the private sector show every sign of being unreconciled and unreconcilable both to the limited reforms that have survived and to the very idea of a political process that enables an electoral majority to inhibit the exercise of financial power or to reduce inequality or even to prevent its aggravation. Since neither the financiers nor the *jefes* nor even the humble foot soldiers of the death squads, employed by elements of the private sector in the early 1980s against reformers and revolutionaries without much apparent discrimination, have been punished, and since attitudes seem unchanged, the assassins remain at hand, ready for use in the event of a more serious challenge from the Left or a relaxation of restraints belatedly imposed by the Reagan administration, under relentless congressional prodding, as a condition of continued aid.

While its continuance assures that the guerrillas will not win, as far as one can tell, they have the number of skilled, disciplined, and committed cadres and sufficient sympathizers in the general population to go on bleeding the economy and frustrating reconstruction, much less development. The military threat they pose discourages investment and encourages the armed forces to depopulate substantial parts of a country that at the best of times has a depressing paucity of land in relation to the number of its people.

As for the Christian Democrats, some say they are inept and corrupt and confused. Others insist that they simply lack the raw power to fulfill their electoral commitments to peace, reconstruction, reform, development, and establishment of the rule of law. Whatever the explanation for these failures, their cumulative effect has been to thwart Christian Democrats' efforts to build a solid base among workers and peasants. In short, the Christian Democrats command neither the armed forces nor an indisputable electoral majority, nor, it is clear, the size, composition, or conditions of U.S. aid. The Reagan administration has, for instance, made clear its hostility to the sort of negotiated power-sharing arrangements that it appears to regard as the minimum requirement for ending its proxy war against Nicaragua.

The one Salvadoran group waxing under the prevailing equilibrium of forces is the officer corps. It now controls troops quadruple the number in place at the start of the decade and, as a consequence of U.S. military assistance, sums of money far greater than those the oligarchy and the national treasury provided before the guerrillas became a serious threat.

*Policy.* As I have understood him, Professor van den Haag has defended the proposition that waging war against the Sandinista government through the medium of the Contras is the only means— other than invasion—for preventing Nicaragua from becoming a totalitarian state wedded to the Soviet Union, i.e., another Cuba. That pessimistic conclusion rests, it seems to me, on insufficient appreciation of Nicaragua's distinctive character, of the diverse trajectories followed by other Marxist-oriented regimes in response to the particularities of domestic conditions and international context, and of the nonmilitary instruments available to the United States and its allies.

The purpose animating Reagan administration policy toward Nicaragua—and El Salvador too, for that matter—has been to win a decisive military victory over the forces of the Left, thereby eliminating them from the political stage for the foreseeable future. Failing that, the minimum goal has been isolation and progressive debilitation of the Sandinista government and the Salvadoran opposition. Because Professor van den Haag has sometimes ignored the particulars of my argument, tending rather to treat my overall position as a typical expression of what he presumes to be liberal thought, I fear that even as we approach the end of our formal discourse, he still misconceives what is and what is not at the heart of my opposition to administration policy.

That opposition does not stem from a categorical rejection of the use of force in international affairs. In the world as it is and as we can expect it to be, eschewing the use of force by yourself is equivalent to inviting its use by others.

Nor does it stem from the view that America should never use the vast and varied means at its disposal to influence the character, as well as the policies, of other states. Our values and our interests are served by the spread of democratic political culture. On this point I may well be more convinced than my colleague. What is at issue is how best to pursue that end, taking into account the full range of national interests and the very problematic nature of the enterprise.

Nor is my opposition nurtured by the belief that third world elites sailing under authoritarian-socialist flags of one sort or another are in general more likely than those extolling the virtues of capitalism to create, whether intentionally or otherwise, conditions conducive either to higher standards of material welfare for the general population or the development of a relatively humane political culture. After the first rising against Somoza, I urged the Carter administration to force the dictator's resignation, not only in order to avoid the horror of a full-scale civil war but also to facilitate multilateral oversight of the succession, to the end of guaranteeing a fair distribution of power among the various constituents of the anti-Somoza coalition and thereby laying the foundation for an authentic democracy. Where I differ with my colleague and the rest of the Right is over their conviction that conservative regimes—however muddled or vicious and regardless of the social, political, and cultural context in which they seek to obtain or retain power—always are preferable from both a strategic and a humanitarian perspective.

Policy for particular cases must begin with what is, not what might have been. Whether I am right that the Carter administration—by committing itself at an early point both to Somoza's departure and dismantlement of the repressive structure created by him, and by conceding that the Sandinistas had earned a share of power—could have rallied a broad front of European and Latin American democracies in favor of an externally guided transition is in the short term academic. It did not, and the Sandinistas, as the only leaders in direct command of troops, occupied the heights of power. Policy must begin with that fact.

Nor can it now ignore the Contra presence and still be deemed responsible. Though made in Washington and still profoundly dependent on Washington's aid and advice, the movement has independent interests and sufficient means for autonomous action to cause a good deal of trouble in Central America if the aid tap were closed without *any* quid pro quo. Moreover, some of its leaders have much to contribute to Nicaraguan political and economic life in the setting of a relatively open and tolerant politics. It would, in addition, be inhumane to confront the movement's foot soldiers with the alternatives of incarceration in Nicaragua, a hopeless fight to the death, or the life of indigent refugees scattered around the region. Central America, and the United States as well, contains enough men skilled in little more than the arts of war.

It is often said of the Soviet Union that it relies principally on weapons to conduct influence-gathering operations in the third world because its other assets are so exiguous. In relation to Nicaragua, the Reagan administration has been acting as if it were equally handicapped; it has largely failed to bring to bear its rich cultural, economic, and diplomatic assets. Rather than seizing the diplomatic initiative, peppering the area with plans for peaceful cooperation and development, it has snapped like an underfed Doberman at the various peace proposals originating among its natural allies in Latin America. It has lunged at anyone attempting to open the door to peace because, as I noted above, its transcendant purpose has been not peace but unambiguous military victory. That purpose being inimical to the ideals and interests of most West European democracies and governments of the democratic or at least pluralist states of Latin America (such as Mexico, Colombia, Venezuela, Costa Rica, Peru, Brazil, and Argentina), we have managed what our adversaries by their best efforts could not have achieved—namely, to effect our diplomatic isolation.

To reassert leadership we must revise our goals. Both our interests and our values would be best served in the present context by relinquishing our obsession with victory and replacing it with the linked goals of tranquilizing Central America and reigniting regionwide economic growth. To achieve these goals we must seek negotiated settlements of the civil conflicts in Nicaragua and El Salvador and concurrent guarantees of mutual tolerance among the Central American states.

There can be no peace in Nicaragua if we attempt to deprive the Sandinistas of control over the country's armed forces. While their opponents, if they lay down their arms and reenter political life, can depend on the threat of U.S. intervention to protect them from betrayal and extermination, the Sandinistas have no comparable security cushion. The Cubans lack the means and the Soviet Union lacks the interest and, in any event, the United States would employ its conventional superiority in the Caribbean Basin to block any effort to save the Sandinistas from betrayal.

Nor is it reasonable to expect the Sandinistas to yield at this time the power they won on the battlefield to set the broad parameters of the Nicaraguan political process. Even in the formally democratic states of Latin America—Colombia, for example—a small and rather homogeneous elite, including in most instances generals of the armed forces, establish the parameters of legal and institutional change. One hopes and to some degree anticipates that as and if democracy deepens in these countries, the elite will grow in size and diversity and will be more responsive to majority will. If, as part of an overall settlement, the Sandinistas open the political process and loosen restraints on party organization and other forms of association, a similar process is likely to occur. The United States can facilitate it by financing cultural ties and economic projects calculated to increase the wealth and status of workers, farmers, and small businessmen.

Together with other interested parties, the United States could provide luxurious incentives for the reintegration of rank-and-file Contras into Nicaraguan society. With respect to those who cannot or are unwilling to return to Nicaragua, the United States could create irresistible financial incentives for Honduras to make a place for them in its underpopulated country and should provide them with the capital and technical training essential if they are to have a fair chance to succeed as farmers, skilled workers, or businessmen.

Since El Salvador's guerrillas have the same survival problem as the Contras but in more aggravated form, a negotiated settlement must include effective guarantees for their security. Those guarantees could assume a variety of forms, all anathema, of course, to the Salvadoran armed forces and the agroindustrial oligarchy, which wants the Left integrated not into the country's politics but rather into its graveyards. Given the structural survival of the right-wing death squads and the triumph of reaction in the armed forces themselves and the failure of Napoleon Duarte to subordinate the military to civilian control, when he and his American sponsors call on the guerrillas to lay down their arms and join the political process, they are inviting them to a rendezvous with death.

Thus, the Left's insistence in its peace proposals on the ceasefire and separation of forces followed by a sharp reduction in the size of the country's armed forces and the integration into them of guerrilla cadres is a reasonable response to their very severe survival problem. Washington need not and, indeed, should not offer its own blueprint for a final settlement. What it needs to do is concede that the Left in El Salvador—which, unlike the Nicaraguan opposition, was not initially fabricated abroad—is at least as legitimate a participant in the political life of El Salvador as the Contras are in the life of Nicaragua, that it has ample reason for seeking security guarantees, and that Washington's support for the armed forces and the economy of El Salvador is going to be conditioned on a good-faith effort to bring the Left into the political process.

El Salvador is not the Philippines, where, because of the size of the country and, in particular, its middle classes and the strength of key institutions like the military and the Catholic Church, the United States played a marginal albeit important role in the quasi-revolutionary upheaval that brought Cory Aquino to power. The United States is the prop of El Salvador's armed forces and its economy. It thus can exercise enormous influence over the armed forces, the oligarchy, and the Christian Democrats. With the stick of threatened withdrawal and the carrot of guarantees against an ultimate seizure of power by the Left, it can overcome resistance to a settlement. If the armed forces are shrunk and ideologically balanced and the Left enters politics, a Center–Left coalition can carry forward the reforms that will truly pacify the country and restore it to the path of sustained economic growth.

On this day, August 5, 1987, the United States has begun its first arguably serious diplomatic initiative since the early years of the Reagan administration. With the properly skeptical cooperation of the Democratic Party's congressional leadership, it has indicated a readiness to talk to the Sandinistas about a settlement under which it would terminate aid to the Contras on condition that Nicaragua ceases to draw military assistance from the Eastern block and opens its politics, so that the Contra leaders can compete on fair terms. Whether this is a ploy to undermine the settlement proposal developed by President Arias of Costa Rica or a serious initiative remains to be seen. Washington could add credibility and psychological weight to its proposal by calling now for parallel negotiations with the Salvadoran opposition. But that, I fear, would be asking too much of this administration. Still, we should celebrate whatever omens it offers us of a willingness to relinquish dreams of military victory at whatever cost in other people's lives and American interests.

Professor van den Haag and I have inevitably rested our respective cases on that collective subjective experience known as "history." From history we have drawn ardently defended hypotheses about the nature of power and influence, the evolutionary tendencies of various political and social organisms, the causes of conflict and misperception, and the means of maximizing human freedom.

It is in the nature of the cases we have made that the "truth" will never be known, although, whatever happens, conflicting accounts of it will no doubt be announced. Therefore, although both of us may be wrong in important features of our clustered predictions about cause and effect, our errors will remain matters of dispute among more and less reasonable people.

Contradictory policies cannot be pursued simultaneously. And the world will not hold still while nations attempt sequential experiments. Nor, of course, is policy a single, simple action seeking a single result with measurable consequences. If, for instance, the Contras were ultimately to achieve military ascendancy and, sometime thereafter, to consolidate a regime amiably responsive to

American interests and able to govern without horrific violations of
human rights, we would still be left to speculate whether the same
end might have been achieved by other means at less cost to the
people of Nicaragua, to other peoples in the region, and to the diverse goals of American foreign policy. One misleads, moreover,
in speaking of an end. History is not a movie. The plot continues to
unfold. Interests and governments change. The costs and benefits
of any action must be perpetually recalculated as history reveals
new possibilities.

In the heat of debate all of us speak with a show of certainty
radically at odds with the contingent character of the human condition. The real policy issue is how to choose in a world where, in the
nature of things, we can know so little about cause and effect. One
of the guidelines I have implicitly proposed is that, at least in cases
that do not involve threats to the supreme strategic interests of the
country, we should limit ourselves to means and ends sanctioned by
a broad international consensus. A second is that, as an enormously
successful nation—where the population enjoys a level of physical
comfort, of security from external attack, and of freedom with few
parallels in human history—the United States should employ means
tending to enhance restraints on the use of force in international
relations.

A third is that policy options that do not command strong congressional support should normally be rejected, both because dis-
sension is a warning of the policy's weak intellectual foundations
and because efforts to implement it will incidentally hamper congressional–executive cooperation in general and will inject venom
into political discourse. A fourth, largely implicit in the preceding
three, is that presidents should regard force as the means of last
resort (recognizing that in exceptional cases it may be the only
means to counter an imminent threat to important interests) and
should treat with skepticism initiatives that do not command the
uncoerced support of our principal allies. A fifth is that where our
policy is animated principally by moral concerns, we should con-

sider the use of force only in an effort to thwart large-scale massacres—taking into account the number of dead and maimed likely to result from our intervention—and, of course, in cases where intervention does not threaten to ignite a general international conflagration. Those are guidelines, not iron laws. They do not preclude the direct or indirect use of force. If the past is prologue, we can anticipate over the next decades new cases of U.S. involvement in armed conflicts of one kind or another. Like all peoples, we will kill and will be killed for the sake of theory. That has been one of the tragedies of human history. I do not anticipate an early end to its long run. One can only hope that the occasions will be few and that the theory will at least express rationally the deepest shared values of our society rather than some sectarian dogma.

# Bibliography

## Central America: General

*Appendix to the Report of the National Bipartisan Commission on Central America* (Washington, DC: U.S. Government Printing Office, 1984).

Phillip Berryman, *Inside Central America* (New York: Pantheon Books, 1985).

Morris J. Blachman, William M. Leogrande, and Kenneth Sharpe, *Confronting Revolution: Security Through Diplomacy in Central America* (New York: Pantheon Books, 1986).

James Chace, "Getting Out of the Central American Maze," *The New York Review* (June 24, 1984), p. 20.

"Country Reports on Human Rights Practices for 1984," submitted to the Committee on Foreign Affairs, House of Representatives, and the Committee on Foreign Relations, U.S. Senate, by the Department of State (Washington, DC: U.S. Government Printing Office, 1985).

"Country Reports on Human Rights Practices for 1985," submitted to the Committee on Foreign Affairs, House of Representatives, and the Committee on Foreign Relations, U.S. Senate, by the Department of State (Washington, DC: U.S. Government Printing Office, 1986).

"Country Reports on Human Rights Practices for 1986," submitted to the Committee on Foreign Affairs, House of Representatives, and the Committee on Foreign Relations, U.S. Senate, by the Department of State (Washington, DC: U.S. Government Printing Office, 1987).

"Critique: Review of the Department of State's Country Reports on Human Rights Practices for 1986," The Watch Committees/Lawyers Committee for Human Rights (New York: Americas Watch, 1987).

Martin Diskin, ed., *Trouble in Our Backyard: Central America and the United States in the Eighties* (New York: Pantheon Books, 1983).

William H. Durham, *Scarcity and Survival in Central America: Ecological Origins of the Soccer War* (Stanford, CA: Stanford University Press, 1979).

Thomas O. Enders, "The Central America Challenge," *AEI Foreign Policy* 4 (2), (1982), p. 8.

Richard R. Fagen and Olga Pellicer, eds., *The Future of Central America: Policy Choices for the U.S. and Mexico* (Stanford, CA: Stanford University Press, 1983).

Tom J. Farer, The Grand Strategy of the United States in Latin America (New Brunswick, NJ: Transactions, 1988).

Tom J. Farer, "Contadora: The Hidden Agenda," *Foreign Policy* 59 (Summer 1985), p. 59.

Richard Feinberg, ed., *Central America: International Dimensions of the Crisis* (New York: Holmes & Meier Publishers, 1982).

Margaret Daly Hayes, "The Stakes in Central America and U.S. Policy Responses," *AEI Foreign Policy* 4 (2) (1982), p. 12.

Robert S. Leiken, ed., *Central America: Anatomy of Conflict*, published in cooperation with Carnegie Endowment for International Peace (New York: Pergamon Press, 1984).

Robert S. Leiken and Barry Rubin, eds., *The Central American Crisis Reader* (New York: Summit Books, 1987).

Charles Maechling, Jr., "Human Rights Dehumanized," *Foreign Policy* 52 (Fall 1983), p. 118.

Richard Millett, "Central American Paralysis," *Foreign Policy* 39 (Summer 1980), p. 99.

David Scott Palmer, "Military Governments and U.S. Policy: General Concerns and Central American Cases," *AEI Foreign Policy* 4 (2) (1982), p. 24.

Robert Pastor, "An 8-Point Peace Plan for Central America," *The Washington Post*, 5 July 1983, p. A19.

Robert Pastor, "Sinking in the Caribbean Basin," *Foreign Affairs* 60 (5) (Summer 1982), p. 1038.

Andrew, J. Pierre, ed., *Central America: Third World Instability as a European–American Issue* (New York: Council on Foreign Relations, 1985).

Susan Purcell, "The Choice in Central America," *Foreign Affairs* 66 (1) (Fall 1987), p. 109.

Susan Kaufman Purcell, "Demystifying Contadora," *Foreign Affairs* 64 (1) (Fall 1985), p. 74.

"The Reagan Administration's Human Rights Record in 1984," Americas Watch Committee (New York: Americas Watch, January 1985).

"The Reagan Administration's Human Rights Record in 1985," Watch Committees/ Lawyers Committee (New York: Americas Watch, January 1986).

"The Reagan Administration's Record on Human Rights in 1986," Watch Committees/ Lawyers Committee (New York: Americas Watch, February 1987).

Carla Anne Robbins, *The Cuban Threat* (New York: McGraw-Hill, 1983).

Steve C. Ropp and James A. Morris, eds., *Central America: Crisis and Adaptation*, (Albuquerque, NM: University of New Mexico Press, 1984).

Max Singer, "Losing Central America," *Commentary* 82 (1) (July 1986), p. 11.

Robert Tucker, "Their Wars, Our Choices," *The New Republic* (24 October 1983), p. 22.

Ernest van den Haag, "The Busyness of American Policy," *Foreign Affairs* 64 (1) (Fall 1985), p. 113.

Howard J. Wiarda, "The Central American Crisis: A Framework for Understanding," *AEI Foreign Policy* 4 (2) (1982), p. 2.

Ralph Lee Woodward, Jr., *Central America: A Nation Divided* (New York: Oxford University Press, 1976).

# El Salvador

Enrique Baloyra, *El Salvador in Transition* (Chapel Hill, NC: University of North Carolina Press, 1982).

Howard I. Blutstein, Elinor C. Betters, John Cobb, Jr., Jonathan A. Leonard, and Charles Townsend, *El Salvador: A Country Study*, Area Handbook Series (Washington, DC: The American University, 1979).

Luis Burstin, "A Night with the FMLN," *Commentary* 79 (5) (May 1985), p. 52.

Shirley Christian, "The Other Side," *The New Republic* (24 October 1983), p. 13.

Joan Didion, "In El Salvador," *The New York Review* (4 November 1982).

Joan Didion, "In El Salvador: Soluciones," *The New York Review* (18 November 1982).

Joan Didion, "El Salvador: Illusions," *The New York Review* (2 December 1982).

"El Salvador's Other Victims: The War on the Displaced," Lawyers Committee for International Human Rights (New York: Americas Watch, 1984).

Mark Falcoff, "The El Salvador White Paper and Its Critics," *AEI Foreign Policy* 4 (2) (1982), p. 18.

Piero Gleijeses, "The Case for Power Sharing in El Salvador," *Foreign Affairs* 61 (5) (Summer 1983), p. 1048.

Leonid Gomez and Bruce Cameron, "El Salvador: The Current Danger: American Myths," *Foreign Policy* 43 (Summer 1981), p. 43.

Robert A. Pastor, "Our Real Interests in Central America," *The Atlantic Monthly* (July 1982), p. 27.

"As Bad As Ever: A Report on Human Rights in El Salvador," Americas Watch Committee with the American Civil Liberties Union (New York: Americas Watch, January 1984).

"Waiting for Justice: Treatment of Political Prisoners Under El Salvador's Decree 50" (Washington DC: International Human Rights Law Group, March 1987).

# Guatemala

"Civil Patrols in Guatemala," Americas Watch Committee (New York: Americas Watch, August 1986).

The Honorable George C. Edwards and William J. Butler, Esq., "Guatemala: A New Beginning" (New York: American Association for the International Commission of Jurists, April 1987).

*Guatemala: The Human Rights Record* (London: Amnesty International Publications, 1987).

"Guatemala Revised: How the Reagan Administration Finds 'Improvements' in Human Rights in Guatemala," Americas Watch Committee (New York: Americas Watch, September 1985).

"Guatemalan Refugees in Mexico, 1980–1984," The Americas Watch Committee (New York: Americas Watch, September 1984).

"Human Rights in Guatemala during President Cerezo's First Year," Americas Watch Committee/British Parliamentary Human Rights Group (New York: Americas Watch, January 1987).

"Little Hope: Human Rights in Guatemala, January 1984–January 1985," Americas Watch Committee (New York: Americas Watch, February 1985).

"The 1985 Guatemalan Elections—Will the Military Relinquish Power?" Report of the Delegation, International Human Rights Law Group and the Washington Office on Latin America, 1985.

Roger Plant, *Guatemala: Unnatural Disaster* (London: The Latin American Bureau, 1978).

"Report on Guatemala," findings of the Study Group on United States–Guatemalan Relations, SAIS Papers in International Affairs, no. 7 (Westview Press/Foreign Policy Institute, 1985).

"A Report on the United Nations Special Rapporteur on Human Rights in Chile, Guatemala, Iran, and Poland," Americas Watch, Asia Watch, and Helsinki Watch Committees (New York: Americas Watch, January 1986).

Stephen Schlesinger and Stephen Kinzer (with an introduction by Harrison Salisbury), *Bitter Fruit* (New York: Doubleday & Co., 1982).

# Honduras

"Human Rights in Honduras: Central America's 'Sideshow,' " Americas Watch Committee (New York: Americas Watch, May 1987).

"With the Miskitos in Honduras," Americas Watch Committee (New York: Americas Watch, April 1986).

# Nicaragua

"Appraisals of the ICJ's Decision: *Nicaragua v. United States (Merits),*" *American Journal of International Law* 81 (1) (January 1987), pp.77–183.

John A. Booth, *The End and the Beginning: The Nicaraguan Revolution* (Boulder, CO:

Westview Press, 1982).

Arturo J. Cruz, "Nicaragua's Imperiled Revolution," *Foreign Affairs* 61 (5) (Summer 1983), p. 1031.

Lloyd N. Cutler, "The Right to Intervene," *Foreign Affairs* 64 (2) (Fall 1985), p. 98.

Christopher Dickey, *With the Contras: A Reporter in the Wilds of Nicaragua* (New York: Simon & Schuster, 1987).

Mark Falcoff, "Nicaraguan Harvest," *Commentary* 80 (1) (July 1985), p. 21.

"Freedom of Expression and Assembly in Nicaragua during the Election Period," Americas Watch Committee (New York: Americas Watch, 1984).

Piero Gleijeses, "Nicaragua: Resist Romanticism," *Foreign Policy* 54 (Spring 1984), p. 122.

David Harowitz, "Nicaragua: A Speech to My Former Comrades on the Left," *Commentary* 81 (6) (June 1986), p. 27.

"Human Rights in Nicaragua 1985–1986," Americas Watch Committee (New York: Americas Watch, March 1986).

"Human Rights in Nicaragua During 1986," Americas Watch Committee (New York: Americas Watch, February 1987).

"Human Rights in Nicaragua: Reagan, Rhetoric and Reality," Americas Watch Committee. (New York: Americas Watch, July 1985).

Penn Kemble and Arturo J. Cruz, Jr., "How the Nicaraguan Resistance Can Win," *Commentary*, 82 (6) (December 1986), p. 19.

Morton Kondracke, "Saving the 'Contras,' " *The New Republic* (29 December 1986), p. 9.

Robert Leiken, "Nicaragua Cliffhanger," *The New Republic* (14 December 1987), p. 17.

"The Miskitos in Nicaragua—1981–1984," Americas Watch Committee (New York: Americas Watch, November 1984).

Jefferson Morley, "Contra Delusion," *The New Republic* (31 March 1986), p. 14.

Joshua Muravchik, "The Nicaragua Debate," *Foreign Affairs* 65 (2) (Winter 1986/1987), p. 366.

"The Nicaragua Debate," *Tikkun* 1 (2) (1985), p. 48.

Robert Pastor, "The Target and the Source: El Salvador and Nicaragua," *Washington Quarterly* 5 (3) (Summer 1982), p. 116.

Stephen S. Rosenfeld, "The Guns of July," *Foreign Affairs* 64 (4) (Spring 1986), p. 698.

Peter Rosset and John Vandermeer, eds., *Nicaragua: Unfinished Revolution* (New York: Grove Press, 1986).

Wayne S. Smith, "Lies About Nicaragua," *Foreign Policy* 67 (Summer 1987), p. 87.

Richard H. Ullman, "At War with Nicaragua," *Foreign Affairs* 62 (1) (Fall 1983), p. 39.

Viron P. Vaky, "Positive Containment in Nicaragua," *Foreign Policy* 68 (Fall 1987), p. 42.

"Violations of the Laws of War by Both Sides in Nicaragua 1981–1985," Americas Watch Committee (New York: Americas Watch, March 1985).

Robert Wesson, "Nicaragua: Reflection on a Journey," *The Center Magazine* (May/June 1984), p. 24.

# Index